Kelsey!

Hope you find Inspiration!

DINNER DÉJÀ

Among my favorite Recipes!

Keep Cooking!

Chef Jennifer

DINNER DÉJÀ VU

Southern Tonight, French Tomorrow

JENNIFER HILL BOOKER

photography by
Deborah Whitlaw Llewellyn

PELICAN PUBLISHING COMPANY
GRETNA 2017

Photography by Deborah Whitlaw Llewellyn
Design and production by Janice Shay / Pinafore Press
Food styling by Jennifer Hill Booker

The word "Pelican" and the depiction of a pelican are
trademarks of Pelican Publishing Company, Inc., and are
registered in the U.S. Patent and Trademark Office.

ISBN: 9781455622924
E-book ISBN: 9781455622931

Printed in China

Published by Pelican Publishing Company, Inc.
1000 Burmaster Street, Gretna, Louisiana 70053

This one is for my Father,
Henry W. Hill, who always
pushes me to be the best…
and to my Mother,
Laverne Scurlock Hill,
who always tells me that
my best is good enough.

I love you both.

CONTENTS

INTRODUCTION

After writing my first cookbook, *Field Peas to Foie Gras: Southern Recipes with a French Accent*, I was thrilled to learn that there are many people who share my love for cooking traditional Southern food, blended with classical French cooking techniques. They know, as I do, that this combination adds a bit of flair to their everyday meals. I also learned that, like me, there are many cooks who dread that weekly trip to the grocery store and need a little encouragement to create fresh new menus, week after week. The inspiration for this cookbook, *Dinner Déjà Vu: Southern Tonight, French Tomorrow*, comes from a desire to reduce my number of trips to the market, save money by buying fewer ingredients, plus it mirrors how I cook for my own family. I prepare two different meals from the same ingredients—usually Southern one night, and French the other. Sometimes I blend both cuisines together in one recipe, which is the case in Pecan Bread Pudding with Crème Anglais (page 157), a favorite dessert of mine.

As a chef, I'm expected to create tasty and exciting meals at work, then come home and prepare another exciting meal for my family— every single night of the week. I do my best to have dinner on the table by 6 p.m., although some nights we may eat as late as 8 p.m. As a single working mother of two, I'm often caught staring into the open refrigerator after a long day, wondering what to cook for dinner. Actually, I'm like most home cooks—I'm usually short of time, energy, and often patience when it comes to planning and cooking family meals.

If this sounds familiar, you'll appreciate this collection of simple and innovative recipes that pairs tasty, traditional Southern dishes with French classics—both using the same basic ingredients. Making multiple dishes using the same ingredients is a trick I've learned over the years to keep everyone excited at meal time. A menu of recipes that use several, if not all, of the same ingredients can result in new and distinctly different— but equally delicious—meals. When standing at the meat counter looking at chicken for dinner, I consider how many different ways I can cook that chicken and keep the meals interesting. Best of all, using the same ingredients to do double duty in the kitchen allows me to prepare a traditional Southern dinner one night and a classic French meal the next—with the added bonus of cutting my shopping and cooking time in half, as well as saving money at the market or grocery.

There are many parallels between traditional

Southern food and rustic French cuisine. I grew up in the South, which has a very long growing season. So we were fortunate ito enjoy lots of fresh produce from our garden most of the year. From a very early age I learned that fruits and vegetables taste best when eaten in their growing season. As an adult, I've learned that seasonal foods taste better because they are picked at their peak of freshness, which makes their flavors bigger and brighter. Fresh-picked is also the healthiest choice.

There is the added bonus of produce being less expensive when purchased in season, mainly because there is so much of it. I remember visiting my grandparents during the summer—by the end of August they were more tomatoes, peppers, and okra than we knew what to do with. My Southern heritage still influences what I eat, and it also influences what I cook in my profession as a Chef, and as a home cook for my family.

Living in Paris and studying French cuisine at Le Cordon Bleu College of Culinary Arts taught me that many French dishes could easily be paired with the Southern dishes I grew up with. French and Southern cooking uses many of the same ingredients, such as poultry and wild game; fresh herbs, such as thyme and sage; and fresh fruits, like apples and figs. You'll find theses shared ingredients in the cassoulets and casseroles, soups and stews, salads and seafood, cakes and cocktail recipes in this cookbook. For example, when I prepare Roasted Chicken with fresh lemon, garlic, and rosemary (page 129) for Sunday dinner

in the French Provencal method, I use the leftover roasted chicken to make a Southern Chicken Pot Pie (page 128) for Monday night's dinner.

Some of the recipes in this cookbook are geared to re-using leftovers—a handy solution for any busy cook. Simple side dishes such as Roasted Sweet Potatoes (page 42) can easily be turned into light and airy Sweet Potato Crepes with Brown Sugar Butter (page 45) for dessert the next night; or fill leftover crepes with Fig Preserves (page 17) for a breakfast treat the next morning.

Other recipes in this book pair French and Southern dishes that use similar ingredients, to make your shopping easier and more budget friendly. For example, take the same ingredients used to make the Fried Creamed Corn (or use some of the extra fried corn), and turn it into a rich and elegant Fresh Corn Bisque (page 41). Creating two different meals—one Southern and one French—using the same ingredients is easy and refreshing.

The same can be said about turning French favorites into traditional Southern dishes. A Cassoulet (page 65), which is a bean and meat stew, can easily be made into a pot of Pinto Beans & Smoked Ham Hocks (page 64); and by doubling up on the oysters you buy to make Roasted Oysters in Champagne (page 87), you'll have enough to make Fried Oysters with Red Pepper Sauce (page 86) the next day. Helping home cooks to shop once and eat twice—while satisfying the craving for both down-home comfort dishes as well as French specialties—is what I hope will make this your must-have cookbook.

I'm often asked how I came to pair Southern and French cuisines, and my answer is always the same: They are two sides of the same coin. What I mean by this is that both cuisines have a rich food history of using fresh local ingredients in their dishes, applying cooking methods that bring out the best flavors of the food, and a special talent for creating dishes that dazzle. People are sometimes surprised with how the same ingredients for the Southern dishes we know and love can also be used to create a little bite of France. Take corn, for example. By cutting the kernels off the cobb and frying it in a cast iron skillet with a little bacon grease or butter, onions, and a splash of cream; you've made Fried Creamed Corn, a dish most Southerners would consider a summer time favorite. For the dessert lovers of the world, imagine making Bourbon Pecan Pie (page 156) and Pecan Bread Pudding with Crème Anglaise (page 157), using many of the same ingredients.

At the back of this cookbook you will find combined grocery lists for each pairing of recipes, so that you can shop once, and eat twice.

The recipes in *Dinner Déjà Vu: Southern Tonight, French Tomorrow* are simply written, with easy to follow instructions. The chapters are peppered with How-To guides to help explain the more detailed recipes; and you will find a chapter of Recipe Basics, which come in handy when you want to make stocks, vinaigrettes, and spice blends. There is a list of Essential Equipment to helps the home cook outfit their kitchen, and will remind the seasoned home cook what kitchen equipment is a "must have." You'll also find a list of items For the Pantry to help you stock many common cooking ingredients; and the Glossary defines French cooking terms that may be unfamiliar.

I truly enjoyed writing this cookbook. My hope is that it will save you time and money, and will be your go-to guide for inspiring meals that are perfect from beginning to end. So whether you feel like Charleston or the Champs Elysees for dinner tonight, know that these recipes will keep you inspired to cook fresh and exciting meals.

brandy and cherries

peppers and apple cider vinegar

lemons, strawberries and sugar

garlic and shallots

yellow and brown mustard seed

tomatoes and onions

★ ★ ★

PICKLES & PRESERVES

∙ ∙

Cornichons & Conserves

⚜ ⚜ ⚜

BREAD & BUTTER PICKLES

Yields 2 pint jars

1 pound (about 8) pickling cucumbers,
   sliced into ¼-inch rounds
1 tablespoon kosher or sea salt
½ cup apple cider vinegar
½ cup white wine vinegar
½ cup dark brown sugar
½ cup sugar
1 tablespoon Pickling Spice (recipe, page 189)

Toss the cucumbers and salt together in a colander and let them drain for 60 minutes.

Rinse the cucumbers thoroughly in cold water and drain for another 30 minutes.

Once excess water has drained from the cucumbers, divide them into two sterilized 16-ounce jars and set aside. You may sterilize the jars and lids in your dishwasher on the hot cycle.

While the cucumbers are draining, combine both the vinegars and the sugars with the pickling spice and 1/3 cup water in a large saucepan over medium-high heat. Stir for 10 minutes, until the sugar dissolves and the mixture comes just to the first boil.

Pour the hot pickling brine over the cucumbers in each jar, leaving ¼-inch space from the rim. Slide a clean rubber spatula or wooden skewer around the inside of each jar to remove any air bubbles. Add additional pickling brine if needed. Wipe the rims with a clean towel, add the sterilized lids and screw on the collars, being careful not to overtighten.

Place the jars in a deep pot with a rack or towel at the bottom of the pot, and add enough water to cover the jars by 2 inches. Cover the pot with a tight fitting lid, bring to a boil over high heat, and boil for 20 minutes.

Turn off the heat, uncover, and leave the jars in the water for 10 minutes to cool.

Remove the jars and place on a cooling rack or kitchen towel to cool undisturbed, for at least 12 hours. A vacuum seal will form as the jars cool. To test the seal, press the center of the lid. If the seal is set, the lid should not flex up and down when pressed.

The pickles are ready to eat after 1 week. The pickles will keep in the refrigerator up to 3 months.

PICKLED VIDALIA ONIONS

Yields about 4 cups

2 large Vidalia or yellow onions, thinly sliced
1 small red onion, thinly sliced
3 large cloves garlic, crushed
5 sprigs fresh thyme
2 cups white wine vinegar
½ cup brown sugar
1 cup sugar
1 tablespoon Pickling Spice (recipe, page 189)
¼ teaspoon red pepper flakes

Place the sliced onions, garlic, and thyme in a glass bowl, and set aside.

Combine the vinegar, 1 cup water, brown sugar, sugar, pickling spice, and the red pepper flakes in a stainless steel saucepan over medium heat, and bring to a boil.

Pour the vinegar mixture over the sliced onions and lightly cover with plastic wrap.

Let it cool to room temperature, then transfer to an airtight container.

The pickled onions will keep in the refrigerator for up to 3 months.

VIDALIA ONIONS

This Southern onion is grown in the south Georgia town of Vidalia. They're only available from late April through mid-July, so the best way to enjoy a Vidalia onion's mild sweet taste all year round is to store them in a cool dark place, or preserve them as a pickle.

TOMATO RELISH

Yields about 3 pints

4 large green tomatoes, halved
2 large ripe tomatoes, halved
2 red bell pepper, halved
3 large yellow onions, peeled and quartered
1½ tablespoons Pickling Spice, (recipe,
   page 189)
2 teaspoons salt
1 to 1½ cups sugar
¾ cup cider vinegar

In a large food processor, coarsely grind the tomatoes, red bell peppers, and onions in batches. Mix in a large bowl to combine.

Line a large colander with a triple layer of cheesecloth, place over a large bowl, and pour in the tomato mixture. Drain for 1 hour. You may save and use the tomato juice for another recipe.

In a large stainless steel stockpot over medium-high heat, combine tomato mixture, pickling spice, salt, sugar, and vinegar. Bring to a boil, reduce the heat to low, and simmer for 15 to 20 minutes, stirring frequently, until the relish begins to thicken.

Remove the saucepan from the heat and ladle the hot relish into 3 sterilized pint jars, leaving ¼-inch space from the rim of the jar. Slide a clean rubber spatula or wooden skewer around the inside of each jar to remove any air bubbles. Wipe the rims with a clean towel, add the sterilized lids, and screw on the collars, being careful not to overtighten.

Place the jars in a deep pot with a rack or towel at the bottom of the pot, and add enough water to cover the jars by 2 inches. Cover the pot with a tight fitting lid, bring to a boil over high heat, and boil for 30 minutes.

Turn off the heat, uncover, and leave the jars in the water for 10 minutes to cool.

Remove the jars and place on a cooling rack or kitchen towel to cool undisturbed, for at least 12 hours. A vacuum seal will form as the jars cool. To test the seal, press the center of the lid. If the seal is set, the lid should not flex up and down when pressed.

Store in a cool dark place. Tomato relish is good for up to 1 year.

FIG PRESERVES

My Aunt Sis had a huge fig tree in her front yard, and when she wasn't at home my sisters, cousins, and I would sneak and eat her figs. Lucky for us we never ate enough to keep her from making her Fig Preserves every year.

Yields about 3 half pints

1½ pounds fresh figs, washed, stems removed
3½ cups sugar
¼ cup fresh lemon juice
1 tablespoon lemon zest

In a large stainless steel saucepan, combine the figs, sugar, ½ cup water, lemon juice, and zest. Bring to a simmer over medium low heat, stirring constantly.

Cover and simmer over low heat for 30 minutes, stirring occasionally.

Remove the cover and continue simmering, stirring frequently, for 45 minutes, or until the mixture thickens and gels. To test, spoon a smal amount onto a cold saucer. If it thickens, it has "set up" and is ready.

Fill 3 sterilized half pint jars with the hot fig preserves, leaving ½-inch space at the top. Wipe jar rims clean, add sterilized lids and screw on the bands.

Slide a clean rubber spatula or wooden skewer around the inside of each jar to remove any air bubbles. Wipe the rims with a clean towel, add the sterilized lids, and screw on the collars, being careful not to overtighten.

Place the jars in a deep pot with a rack or towel at the bottom of the pot, and add enough water to cover the jars by 2 inches. Cover the pot with a tight fitting lid, bring to a boil over high heat, and boil for 10 minutes.

Turn off the heat, uncover, and leave the jars in the water for 10 minutes to cool.

Remove from water, wipe dry and store in a cool dark place for up to 6 months.

RED PEPPER SAUCE

Yields 6 to 8 pints

1 pound fresh cayenne peppers,
  stems removed
6 large cloves garlic, smashed
2 cups cider vinegar
1 cup white vinegar
2 tablespoons pickling salt
1 tablespoon sugar

Place the cayenne peppers, garlic, and 2 cups water in a food processor, and pulse until the peppers are pureed. Set aside.

In a medium stainless steel saucepan, bring the vinegar, salt, and sugar to a boil; stirring to dissolve the sugar and salt.

Add the pureed peppers, reduce the heat to low, and simmer for 3 to 5 minutes

Remove from heat and pour into sterilized glass jars or bottles.

Seal tightly with a sterilized lid.

Cool at room temperature and store the jars of pepper sauce in the refrigerator for up to 1 year. Be sure to prepare this hot sauce in a well ventillated area. Note: The longer it sits, the hotter the pepper sauce will be.

STRAWBERRY LAVENDER PRESERVES

Yields about 4 pints

**5 pounds (about 20 cups) fresh strawberries,
  hulled and quartered**
3 cups sugar
½ cup fresh lemon juice
6 tablespoons pectin
2 teaspoons fresh lemon zest
1 tablespoon fresh lavender blooms

Combine the strawberries and sugar in a large stainless steel saucepan, cover, and set aside for 2 hours at room temperature.

After 2 hours, gradually stir in the lemon juice and pectin.

Transfer to the stovetop and slowly bring the mixture to a full rolling boil over medium-high heat, stirring constantly until the sugar has completely dissolved.

Reduce the temperature to medium-low.

Stir in the lemon zest and lavender and simmer 20 minutes, until the mixture thickens. Test the thickness by spooning a small amount onto a cold saucer. The preserves should thicken as it cools. If it doesn't thicken, continue cooking a few more minutes, then retest.

Stir to prevent sticking, scraping down the sides of the pot, and skim off foam as necessary.

Remove the saucepan from the heat and ladle the hot preserves into 4 sterilized pint jars, leaving ¼-inch space from the rim of the jar. Slide a clean rubber spatula or wooden skewer around the inside of each jar to remove any air bubbles. Wipe the rims with a clean towel, add the sterilized lids, and screw on the collars, being careful not to overtighten.

Place the jars in a deep pot with a rack or towel at the bottom of the pot, and add enough water to cover the jars by 2 inches. Cover the pot with a tight fitting lid, bring to a low boil over medium-high heat, and boil for 10 minutes.

Turn off the heat, uncover, and leave the jars in the water for 10 minutes to cool.

Remove the jars and place on a cooling rack or kitchen towel to cool undisturbed, for at least 12 hours. A vacuum seal will form as the jars cool. To test the seal, press the center of the lid. If the seal is set, the lid should not flex up and down when pressed.

Store in a cool dark place for up to 6 months.

PICKLED TOMATOES

Yields 2 (1-pint) jars

1 cayenne pepper, halved lengthwise
1 bay leaf
¼ cup Picking Spice, (recipe, page 189)
3 cloves garlic
2 cups cider vinegar
1 tablespoon dark brown sugar
1 tablespoon kosher salt
1 pound (4 medium) green tomatoes,
  cut into wedges

Combine the cayenne pepper, bay leaf, pickling spice, garlic, vinegar, brown sugar, salt, and 1 cup water in a large saucepan over medium-high heat.

Bring to a boil and cook for 5 minutes. Remove from the heat and let it cool slightly.

Pack the tomatoes into 2 sterilized pint jars.

Pour the hot pickling brine over the tomatoes in each jar, leaving ¼-inch space from the rim. Slide a clean rubber spatula or wooden skewer around the inside of each jar to remove air bubbles. Wipe the rims with a clean towel, add the sterilized lids and screw on the collars, being careful not to overtighten.

Place the jars in a deep pot with a rack or towel at the bottom of the pot, and add enough water to cover the jars by 2 inches. Cover the pot with a tight fitting lid, bring to a low boil over medium-high heat, and boil for 10 minutes.

Turn off the heat, uncover, and leave the jars in the water for 10 minutes to cool.

Remove the jars and place on a cooling rack or kitchen towel to cool undisturbed, for at least 12 hours. A vacuum seal will form as the jars cool. To test the seal, press the center of the lid. If the seal is set, the lid should not flex up and down when pressed.

Store in a cool dry place for up to 1 year, although the tomatoes are at their peak in about 3 months.

SHALLOT & BLACK PEPPERCORN CHAMPAGNE VINEGAR

Yields about 2 pints

2 cups Champagne vinegar
3 shallots, peeled and quartered
1 tablespoon peppercorns
1 large clove garlic, smashed

GARNISH
1 shallot, thinly sliced
1 teaspoon peppercorns

Heat the vinegar in a medium saucepan over medium-low heat. Add the shallots, peppercorns, and garlic and bring to a simmer.

Remove from the heat and pour the vinegar into a sterilized quart jar, making sure to add the shallots, peppercorns, and garlic as well.

Store the jar in a cool, dark place, undisturbed, for 2 weeks.

Strain the vinegar through a cheesecloth into a clean large bowl, and discard the shallots, peppercorns, and garlic.

Using a funnel, pour the vinegar into a sterilized, 16-ounce bottle and garnish with additional sliced shallots and peppercorns.

The vinegar may be used up to 1 year.

VINEGARS

Apple Cider Vinegar
Made from pressed apples that are allowed to ferment to alcohol, and then to vinegar.

Balsamic
A dark brown vinegar, traditionally made in Italy from unfiltered, unfermented grape juice (instead of fermented alcohol), and is aged like wine.

Champagne Vinegar
Champagne vinegar is made from Champagne and has a lighter, fresher taste than other wine vinegars.

Distilled (White) Vinegar
This is made from distilled alcohol that is fermented and most commonly used for making pickles and condiments.

Red Wine Vinegar
This vinegar is made from red wine that is allowed to ferment and has a more acidic flavor than other wine vinegars.

Sherry Vinegar
Made from a fortified Spanish wine and aged for at least six months in oak barrels before being bottled.

White Wine Vinegar
Made from white wine, with a more mellow flavor than red wine or sherry vinegars.

VEGETABLES
·······································
Légumes

⚜ ⚜

PIMENTO CHEESE STUFFED POTATOES

Serves 8

PIMENTO CHEESE SPREAD

4 ounces cream cheese, softened

½ cup mayonnaise

¾ cup extra-sharp cheddar cheese, shredded

½ cup mild cheddar cheese, shredded

¼ cup hickory-smoked bacon, cooked and
   cut into ¼-inch pieces

1 tablespoon onion, minced

1 large clove garlic, minced

1 teaspoon smoked paprika

¼ teaspoon cayenne pepper

¼ cup diced pimento, plus 2 tablespoons
   diced pimentos, for garnish

Salt and freshly ground pepper, to taste

2 tablespoons butter, softened

3 pounds Russet potatoes, peeled, and cut
   into 1/8-inch-thick rounds

To make the Pimento Cheese Spread: Mix the cream cheese and mayonnaise in a large bowl. Add the remaining ingredients and mix until well combined. Adjust to taste with salt and black pepper. Set aside.

Preheat the oven to 400°F.

Lay the potato rounds out on a clean work surface and add a layer of pimento cheese spread to each slice. Generously butter a large 10-inch, or two 8-inch, cast-iron skillets. Shingle the slices in a circle around the skillet, so that they overlap. Sprinkle generously with salt and pepper.

Bake uncovered for 30 minutes, then reduce the temperature to 350*F and bake and additional 30 minutes, until the potatoes are fork tender and the top is golden brown.

Remove from the oven and let it cool for 10 minutes.

Sprinkle with the diced pimentos and serve.

SOUTHERN ICON: PIMENTO CHEESE

What do Southerners and the French have in common? A strong abiding love of CHEESE!

While the French are known for their after-dinner cheeses, we Southerners are famous for our pimento cheese spread.

Although there is some debate to where pimento cheese spread got its start, it is now a Southern staple that graces many a dining room table.

If asked why it's so popular, I would say that's because each batch is as unique as the person making it. Although the base for all pimento cheese spreads is the same—a traditional blend of shredded cheddar cheeses, cream cheese, and roasted red bell peppers—you can make it your own by adding additional ingredients. Want it spicier? Add cayenne pepper. Like your pimento cheese spread extra creamy? Add cream cheese, mayonnaise, AND sour cream.

In my case, I like a smoky heat so smoked paprika and crispy hickory-smoked bacon makes my cheese spread pretty popular among bacon lovers.

While pimento cheese spread's taste will grab your attention, its versatility will keep you coming back for more. It's the perfect substitute for butter when smeared over a hot buttermilk biscuit; a healthier alternative to chips and dip when eaten with fresh cut vegetables; and it's a guaranteed crowd-pleaser at your next potluck dinner.

Macaroni au Gratin

Known in the South as Mac & Cheese, this recipe gives you another version of a beloved dish.

Serves 6

4 ounces thick cut hickory-smoked bacon, cut into ¼-inch lardons
1 tablespoon kosher salt
2 cups dried elbow macaroni
2 tablespoons unsalted butter + 1 tablespoon for the casserole dish
2 tablespoons all-purpose flour
1½ cups milk
4 ounces Gruyere cheese, grated
6 ounces extra-sharp cheddar cheese, grated
1 teaspoon salt
¼ teaspoon freshly ground pepper
Pinch fresh grated nutmeg
½ cup fresh bread crumbs

Butter a 9x13-inch casserole dish with 1 tablespoon butter and set aside.

Heat a large sauté pan over medium heat, add the lardons and cook for 15 minutes, until brown. Remove and drain on a paper towel-lined plate, reserve for later. Set pan aside to use later.

In a large stock pot over medium-high heat, bring 2 quarts water and 1 tablespoon kosher salt to a rolling boil. Add the pasta and cook for 8 to 10 minutes, until firm but tender.

Drain the pasta and pour into the buttered casserole dish.

Preheat an oven to 350°F.

Melt the remaining butter in the pan with the bacon grease over low heat. Once the butter has stopped foaming, whisk in the flour. Cook for 2 minutes, whisking constantly.

Heat the milk in a small saucepan over medium-low heat, but do not boil.

Whisk the hot milk into the flour mixture, and cook for 1 additional minute over low heat, stirring, until the roux is thick and smooth. Be careful not to brown.

Whisk in the Gruyere and cheddar cheese, the salt, pepper, and nutmeg, and stir until smooth. Stir in the lardons and pour over the pasta.

Sprinkle with the bread crumbs and bake for 35 to 40 minutes, or until the sauce is bubbly and the bread crumbs have browned.

Serve hot.

BEET SALAD *with Walnuts, Roquefort & Citrus Vinaigrette*

Serves 8

**4 medium red beets, with root and 1-inch
   stem intact**
**4 medium golden beets, with root and 1-inch
   stem intact**
¼ cup olive oil

CITRUS VINAIGRETTE
Juice of 3 oranges (about ¾ cup)
½ teaspoon local honey
1 large shallot (about 1 tablespoon), minced
2 tablespoons white wine vinegar
½ teaspoon salt
½ teaspoon freshly ground pepper
¼ cup extra-virgin olive oil

½ cup toasted walnuts, chopped
2 ounces Roquefort cheese

Preheat the oven to 400°F.
   Scrub the beets with a brush. Line a roasting pan with foil and coat the foil with olive oil. Add the beets to the pan, turning to coat with the oil. Bake at 400°F for 1 hour, or until the beets are fork tender.

Let the beets cool slightly, then trim off the roots and stems, and peel off the skins.

Cut the beets into wedges ½-inch thick. Place on a platter and set aside.

To make the Citrus Vinaigrette: In a small saucepan over medium heat, bring the orange juice and honey to a boil. Cook for 15 minutes, stirring often, until the liquid has reduced to 4 tablespoons.

Pour into a medium bowl and let it cool slightly. Then add the shallots, vinegar, ½ teaspoon salt, and ¼ teaspoon pepper, and stir with a whisk to combine. Gradually add the oil, whisking constantly. Adjust to taste with salt and pepper.

Drizzle the citrus vinaigrette over the beets and top with the toasted walnuts and Roquefort cheese. Serve warm or at room temperature.

Roasted Beets & Orange Supremes

Serves 8

**4 medium red beets, with root and 1-inch
 stem intact**
**4 medium golden beets, with root and 1-inch
 stem intact**
¼ cup olive oil

ORANGE SUPREMES
4 navel oranges (supreme technique follows)
Salt and freshly ground pepper
¼ cup extra-virgin olive oil

Preheat the oven to 400°F.

Scrub the beets with a brush. Line a roasting pan with foil and coat the foil with olive oil. Add the beets to the pan, turning to coat with the oil. Bake at 400°F for 1 hour, or until the beets are fork tender.

Let the beets cool slightly, then trim off the roots and stems, and peel off the skins.

Cut the beets into ¼-inch thick rounds, and divide between 8 plates, or on a large platter.

To make the Orange Supremes: Cut off both the ends of the fruit, the stem end and the navel end.

On a cutting board, stand the orange on the cut stem end and use a sharp paring knife to slice off the peel and pith, cutting large strips from top to bottom. Do not cut straight down, but follow the contours of the fruit to waste as little of the flesh as possible. Rotate the orange and repeat this process until all the peel is removed and you have a juicy orange sphere.

With a dinner fork, secure the peeled orange on the cutting board, cut out the citrus segments from in between the strips of membrane surrounding them. Lift out each segment and place on the cutting board; remove any seeds. Once the entire orange has been segmented, squeeze any remaining juices from the leftover membranes over the beets.

Arrange the orange supreme segments around the sliced beets. Liberally season with salt and pepper, and drizzle with oil.

Serve chilled or at room temperature.

potatoes

eggs

butter

black pepper

black peppercorns

nutmeg

heavy cream

How to Make Duchess Potatoes

1. Dry the boiled potatoes in a hot oven.

2. Mash thoroughly.

3. Add butter and cream.

4. Add a smooth tip to the pastry bag.

5. Fill the piping bag half full.

6. Pipe in a circular motion.

7. Make each Duchess potato equal size.

8. Brush with the egg wash.

9. Bake until golden brown.

BUTTERMILK WHIPPED POTATOES

Serves 6

4 pounds (about 6 cups) Yukon Gold potatoes, peeled and diced
2 tablespoons salt
½ cup milk
8 tablespoons unsalted butter
½ to 1 cup buttermilk
Salt and freshly ground pepper, to taste

In a large stock pot over high heat, bring 4 quarts water, the diced potatoes, and 2 tablespoons of salt to a boil. Reduce the heat to medium-low and simmer, uncovered, for 10 to 15 minutes, or until the potatoes fall apart easily when pierced with a fork.

Heat the milk and butter in a small saucepan over low heat, but do not boil. Set aside.

Once the potatoes are tender, drain them in a colander; do not rinse.

Place a food mill fitted with the small disk attachment over a bowl and press the potatoes through the food mill, in batches. (You can also use a potato masher, or an electric mixer fitted with the whip attachment.)

Stir the hot milk-and-butter mixture into the potatoes, stir in ½ cup buttermilk, and add more if needed to make the potatoes creamy.

Adjust the seasoning with the salt and pepper, and serve hot.

Duchess Potatoes

When making Duchess Potatoes be sure to allow the boiled potatoes at least 10 minutes drying time in a hot oven.

Makes about 3 dozen

5 pounds Russet potatoes, peeled and diced
2 tablespoons salt
8 egg yolks
8 tablespoons butter, room temperature
¼ teaspoon nutmeg
¾ cup heavy cream
Salt and freshly ground pepper, to taste
1 whole egg
2 tablespoons cream

Preheat the oven to 375°F.

Line 2 baking sheets with parchment paper.

In a large stock pot over high heat, bring 4 quarts water, the diced potatoes, and 2 table-spoons of salt to a boil. Reduce the heat to low and simmer uncovered for 10 to 15 minutes, or until the potatoes fall apart easily when pierced with a fork.

Once the potatoes are tender, drain them in a colander; do not rinse.

Pour the boiled potatoes on the lined baking sheet and place in the preheated oven for 10 to 15 minutes, until the surface of the potatoes have dried slightly.

Place a food mill fitted with the small disk attachment over a bowl and press the potatoes through the food mill, in batches. Let it cool in the bowl for about 5 minutes.

Add the egg yolks, butter, nutmeg, and ¾ cup cream. Stir with a rubber spatula to combine. Add salt and pepper, to taste.

See step-by-step photos for How-to Make Duchess Potatoes, page 31.

Transfer the potato mixture to a large pastry bag fitted with a star tip, and pipe in a circular/upward spiral motion onto the second prepared baking sheet. Refrigerate the baking pan of Duchess Potatoes for 30 minutes.

In a small bowl, whip together 1 egg and 2 tablespoons cream.

Remove the potatoes from the refrigerator and lightly brush each piped potato with the egg wash.

Bake for 10 minutes, until golden brown around the edges. Serve hot or at room temperature.

GRILLED SUMMER ZUCCHINI, SQUASH & ONIONS

Having been brought up on overcooked squash and onions, I'm excited by how a hot grill enhances the flavor of the vegetables while keeping them crisp.

Serves 6

2 tablespoons apple cider vinegar
2 tablespoons fresh lemon juice
3 large cloves garlic (about 1 tablespoon), minced
2 teaspoons chopped fresh thyme leaves
Salt and freshly ground pepper
½ cup olive oil
3 large zucchini, trimmed, and sliced diagonally into ¼-inch slices
5 large yellow crookneck squash, trimmed, and sliced diagonally into ¼-inch slices
2 large red onions, peeled, and cut into ¼-inch rings

Whisk the vinegar, lemon juice, garlic, and thyme together in a large stainless steel bowl until well combined. Season with the salt and pepper, to taste.

Gradually whisk in the oil.

Transfer ¼ cup of the marinade to a small bowl and set aside.

Put the zucchini, yellow squash, and onions in a large casserole dish and pour in the remaining marinade to coat. Cover and marinate at room temperature at least 4 hours, or refrigerate up to 1 day.

Oil the grill grate and heat the grill to 400°F.

Grill the vegetables for 5 to 7 minutes on each side, until they are golden brown and crisp around the edges.

Transfer the vegetables to a platter and drizzle with the reserved marinade.

This dish is good served hot, at room temperature, or even chilled.

Ratatouille with Fresh Cottage Cheese

Serves 6

1 cup tomato paste
1 small onion, diced, about ½ cup
12 large cloves (about ¼ cup) garlic, minced
4 tablespoons olive oil + more to oil the
  parchment
2 cups Vegetable Stock (recipe, page 185)
Salt and freshly ground pepper, to taste
1 small eggplant, trimmed, and cut into
  ¼-inch rounds
1 zucchini, trimmed, and cut into ¼-inch
  rounds
1 yellow squash, trimmed, and cut into
  ¼-inch rounds
1 red bell pepper, seeded and cored, and cut
  into ¼-inch strips
1 yellow bell pepper, seeded and cored, and
  cut into ¼-inch strips
1 teaspoon fresh thyme leaves

GARNISH
1 cup fresh cottage cheese, chilled

Preheat the oven to 375°F.

Cut a piece of parchment paper to fit inside a 9x13-inch baking dish, and use 1 teaspoon olive oil to oil the parchment. Set the parchment aside.

In a large bowl, mix the tomato paste, onion, garlic, 1 tablespoon olive oil, and the vegetable stock until thoroughly combined. Season with salt and pepper to taste, and spread in the bottom of the baking dish.

Arrange alternating slices of eggplant, zucchini, yellow squash, red bell pepper, and yellow bell pepper, starting at the outer edge of the dish and working clockwise towards the center of the dish, overlapping the slices so that a bit of each vegetable's color shows.

Drizzle the vegetables with the remaining 3 tablespoons olive oil, season with salt and black pepper to taste, and sprinkle with the thyme leaves.

Cover the vegetables with the oiled parchment paper, oil-side down, tucking the edges inside the dish, and bake in the preheated oven for 45 minutes, until the vegetables are roasted and tender.

Serve with chilled cottage cheese.

BAKED OMELET *with Spring Vegetables*

Similar to a French quiche, but without the crust. Simply mix all the ingredients together and bake for a quick meal anytime.

Serves 6

1 tablespoon unsalted butter, room temperature
½ pound green asparagus, cut into 1-inch pieces
½ pound white asparagus, cut into 1-inch pieces
2 tablespoons extra-virgin olive oil
1 large bunch green onions, thinly sliced
2 small zucchini (about 2 cups), thinly sliced
¾ cup fresh peas
Salt and freshly ground pepper to taste
8 ounces Swiss cheese, shredded
2 tablespoons thyme leaves
2 tablespoons flatleaf parsley, coarsely chopped
12 large eggs
1 cup heavy cream
¼ teaspoon red pepper flakes

Preheat the oven to 350°F.

Coat a 1½-quart baking dish with 1 tablespoon butter, and set aside.

In a large saucepan, bring 1 quart water and 1 tablespoon salt to a rolling bowl. Blanch the asparagus for 2 minutes, until crisp-tender.

Drain and transfer the asparagus to a bowl of ice water to cool quickly. Drain and set aside.

In a large stainless-steel skillet, heat the olive oil over medium heat. Add the onion and zucchini, season with salt and pepper, and cook for 8 to 10 minutes, until the vegetables have softened. Stir in the asparagus and peas and cook 5 minutes, until just heated through.

Transfer the vegetables to a plate to cool slightly.

Spread the vegetables in the buttered baking dish. Evenly sprinkle with the cheese, thyme, and parsley and set aside.

In a large bowl, whisk the eggs, cream and red pepper flakes for 5 minutes, until light and fluffy. Season with salt and pepper.

Pour the egg mixture over the vegetables and cheese. Bake in the preheated oven for 40 to 45 minutes, until golden brown and the omelet wiggles slightly when the pan is jiggled.

Remove and cool for 10 to 15 minutes before serving. Serve warm or at room temperature.

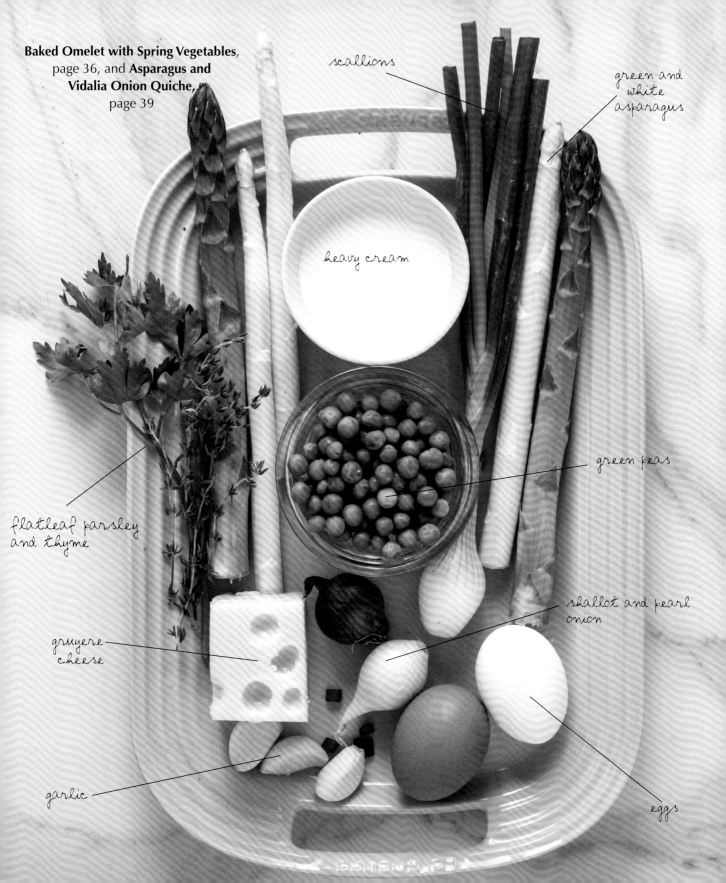

Baked Omelet with Spring Vegetables, page 36, and **Asparagus and Vidalia Onion Quiche,** page 39

scallions

green and white asparagus

heavy cream

flatleaf parsley and thyme

green peas

gruyere cheese

shallot and pearl onion

garlic

eggs

Asparagus & Vidalia Onion Quiche

Serves 6 to 8

1 Quiche Crust (recipe, page 182)

FILLING
2 tablespoons unsalted butter
2 tablespoons olive oil
2 large Vidalia onions, thinly sliced
Salt and freshly ground pepper, to taste
**½ pound fresh thin green asparagus, trimmed
  and cut into 2-inch pieces**
**½ pound fresh thin white asparagus, trimmed
  and cut into 2-inch pieces**
1 teaspoon fresh chopped thyme leaves

CUSTARD
8 large eggs, room temperature
8 ounces heavy cream
1 tablespoon all-purpose flour
1 cup grated Gruyere cheese
½ teaspoon salt
½ teaspoon freshly ground pepper

Prepare a quiche crust according to the recipe.

To make the Filling: Heat a large sauté pan over medium heat and add 1 tablespoon butter and 1 tablespoon olive oil. When the butter stops foaming, add the onions and season with salt and pepper. Cook for 20 minutes, or until the onions are very soft and beginning to brown. Remove the onions from the pan and set aside in a medium bowl.

Add the remaining butter and oil to the same pan. Add the green and white asparagus and sauté for 5 minutes. Remove the pan from the heat, stir in the fresh thyme, and add this mixture to the onions. Set aside to cool.

Preheat the oven to 375°F.

To make the Custard: In a large bowl, whisk together the eggs, cream, and 1 tablespoon flour until well combined. Stir in the grated cheese, salt, and pepper.

Spread the cooled onion and asparagus mixture in the quiche shell and pour the custard mixture over the vegetables.

Bake for about 30 minutes, or until the filling feels firm to the touch.

Place on a cooling rack and cool for at least 15 minutes before slicing and serving.

FRIED CREAMED CORN

A cast-iron skillet is a must when making this dish. It adds a depth of flavor that stainless steel just can't match.

Serves 6

12 ears corn, shucked
4 tablespoons bacon fat, or olive oil
4 tablespoons unsalted butter
**6 scallions (about 1/3 cup), both white and
    green parts, chopped**
Salt and freshly ground pepper, to taste
4 tablespoons all-purpose flour
¼ cup heavy cream

Using a chef knife, slice the corn from the cob into a medium bowl. If you plan to make the Fresh Corn Bisque (recipe, page 41), reserve 6 of the cobs for that dish.

Then scrape the cob downward, using the back of the knife, to get the corn "milk" from the cob into the bowl. Set aside.

In a large cast-iron skillet over medium-high heat, melt the bacon fat and butter. When the bacon fat is hot and the butter has stopped foaming, add the corn, corn milk, and scallions. Add salt and pepper to taste.

Lower the heat to medium-low and cook for 15 to 20 minutes, stirring often.

Stir in the flour 1 tablespoon at a time. When all of the flour has been added, cook an additional 10 minutes, stirring often.

Stir in the heavy cream and cook until just heated through, then adjust the seasoning.

Serve hot. If you plan on making the Fresh Corn Bisque, reserve half (about 3 cups) of the Fried Cream Corn for that recipe.

Fresh Corn Bisque

Slow-cooking the corn brings out its natural sweetness; and warm cream adds sophistication to this summer staple.

Serves 6

6 corn cobs
2 large Russet potatoes (about 2 cups), peeled and diced
3 cups Fried Creamed Corn (recipe, page 40)
Salt and freshly ground pepper, to taste
2 cups heavy cream

GARNISH
1 tablespoon fresh thyme leaves

Put the corn cobs and 6 cups water in a large stock pot and bring to a boil over medium-high heat. Reduce the temperature to medium, and simmer for 20 minutes.

Strain and return the corn stock to the pot, discarding the corn cobs.

Add the diced potatoes to the corn stock, bring to a boil over medium-high heat, then reduce the heat to medium-low and simmer for 20 additional minutes until the potatoes are fork tender.

Add 3 cups Fried Creamed Corn, return to a simmer, and cook another 10 minutes.

Allow the bisque to cool slightly, then use an immersion blender to purée the bisque in the stock pot; or process the soup in batches using a blender or food processor.

Place a fine sieve over a medium bowl and strain the bisque, pressing on the corn and potato solids with the back of a spoon or ladle to remove all of the liquid. Discard the solids.

Heat the heavy cream in a small saucepan over medium heat just until hot. Do not allow it to boil.

Return the bisque to the stock pot, stir in the hot cream, and adjust the seasoning with salt and pepper. Rewarm over low heat for 5 minutes.

Serve in heated bowls and garnish with the fresh thyme.

ROASTED SWEET POTATOES

One of the best things about baked sweet potatoes is that they are so naturally sweet that the only thing they need is a little bit of butter.

Serves 4

5 medium sweet potatoes
1 tablespoon vegetable oil, or lard
4 tablespoons unsalted butter

Preheat the oven to 350°F.

Scrub the sweet potatoes under cool water, and wipe dry.

Brush each sweet potato with oil, arrange on a sheet pan, and bake for 45 minutes to 1 hour, until the sweet potatoes are fork tender.

Cut a slit down the length of each potato. Holding the potato at each end, press towards the middle until the filling pushes up out of the skin.

Top with butter and serve piping hot.

Tips

Sweet potatoes are native to Central and South America, and are one of the oldest vegetables known to man.
Choose sweet potatoes that are firm and without cracks, bruises, or soft spots. Store in a cool, dark, well-ventilated place, and they will keep fresh for ten days. Sweet potatoes should not be stored in the refrigerator because cold temperatures negatively alter their taste.

sweet potatoes

buttermilk

vanilla bean

flour

brown sugar

eggs

butter

Sweet Potato Crepes *with Brown Sugar Butter*

*This Southern spin on a French classic is a flavorful way to use leftover roasted
sweet potatoes. If you have leftover brown sugar butter, it's delicious on muffins, waffles,*

Yields about 3 dozen crepes

CREPES
½ cup mashed Roasted Sweet Potatoes
  (recipe, page 42), skins removed
2 large eggs, beaten
1 to 1½ cups whole milk
1 cup all-purpose flour
4 tablespoons melted butter + more for
  coating the pan
1 pinch salt

BROWN SUGAR BUTTER
Yields 2 (8-ounce) logs

1 pound butter, room temperature
½ cup brown sugar
½ teaspoon cinnamon
½ teaspoon vanilla extract

Combine all the crepe ingredients in a large
bowl with 1/2 cup water and whisk for 10 minutes, until smooth and free of lumps.

Place the crepe batter in the refrigerator and
chill for 1 hour. This allows the air bubbles in
the batter to subside so the crepes will be less
likely to tear during cooking.

Heat an 8-inch, non-stick crepe pan over
medium heat, until the pan is hot but not
smoking.

Use about 1 teaspoon butter to coat the pan.

Pour 1 ounce of the batter into the center of the
pan and swirl to spread evenly.

Cook for 30 seconds, then remove the pan
from the stovetop. Using a rubber spatula,
quickly loosen the edges of the batter from the
pan then, using your hands, very carefully flip
the crepe over.

Place the pan back on the stove and cook
the crepe for another 30 seconds, then use a
rubber spatula to transfer the crepe to a parchment-lined baking sheet. Continue until all
batter is used, or refrigerate leftover batter for
up to 2 days.

After the crepes have cooled, you can fill
them with your choice of fillings, or serve
warm with Brown Sugar Butter.

To make the Brown Sugar Butter: Cut the
butter into chunks. Place the butter and ½ cup
brown sugar into the bowl of a stand mixer fitted with a paddle attachment, and beat at low
speed, just until combined.

Add the cinnamon and vanilla extract, and
increase the speed to medium. Beat for 5 minutes, until well combined.

Spoon the butter onto parchment paper, or
plastic wrap that is large enough to use as a
wrapping. Roll into a log, secure the ends, and
refrigerate for at least 1 hour before using.

BRAISED COLLARD GREENS

I grew up eating collard greens at least once a week while they were in season. I loved drinking the braising liquid, or "pot likker," once all the greens were eaten.

Serves 8

2 smoked ham hocks
4 ounces salt pork
1 cup diced onion (1 large onion)
2 bay leaves
¼ teaspoon red pepper flakes
2 tablespoons white sugar
1 tablespoon apple cider vinegar
2 quarts Chicken Stock (recipe, page 185)
2 large bunches collard greens, washed,
  stemmed, and thinly sliced
Salt and freshly ground pepper, to taste

Place ham hocks, salt pork, onion, bay leaves, red pepper flakes, sugar, vinegar, and chicken stock in a large stockpot over medium-high heat. Bring to a boil, place a tight fitting lid on the stockpot and reduce the heat to low. Simmer for 1 hour.

Add the collard greens, return the lid to the pot, and bring to a boil over medium-high heat. Reduce the heat again to low and simmer for 1 hour, or until the greens are tender. Adjust the seasoning with salt and pepper to taste.

Leftover pot likker tastes great served with Buttermilk Cornbread (recipe, page 112).

Types of Greens

Collard greens are mild, earthy, and have a strong, vegetable flavor. Mustard greens are the greens of the mustard plant, and have a sharp, bright flavor similar to green mustard seeds. Turnip greens are the green tops of turnips and have a mild turnip flavor.

Collard Greens Salad with *Champagne Vinaigrette*

Brighten up your winter with collard greens and a splash of Champagne and a drizzle of decadently delicious pecan oil.

Serves 8

2 bunches collard greens, washed
1 cup pecan oil
2 teaspoon sea salt
½ cup Shallot and Black Peppercorn
  Champagne Vinegar (recipe, page 21)
4 cloves garlic, minced
2 teaspoon red pepper flakes
1 teaspoon freshly ground pepper
1 large onion, thinly sliced
2 large red bell peppers, stemmed, seeded,
  and cut into thin strips

De-stem and chiffonade the collard greens into long strips and place into a large bowl.

Pour the pecan oil on the collard greens and sprinkle with salt. Use your hands to massage the oil and salt into the greens for 5 to 7 minutes, until all pieces are well coated. (Massaging the greens helps to break down their tough fibers and makes them tender.) Set aside.

To make the Champagne Vinaigrette: Whisk together the Champagne Vinegar, the garlic, red pepper flakes, and black pepper.

Pour the Champagne Vinaigrette over the collard greens and marinate in the refrigerator for at least 4 hours, or overnight.

Add the onions and red pepper strips and toss before serving.

HOPPIN' JOHN

Serves 6 to 8

1 tablespoon olive oil
¼ pound thick cut bacon, cut into ¼-inch thick lardons
1 large onion, diced (about 1 cup)
4 celery stalks, diced (about ½ cup)
1 small green pepper, stemmed, seeded and diced (about 1 cup)
3 large cloves garlic, minced
1 pound black-eyed peas, soaked overnight, then drained
6 cups Chicken or Vegetable Stock (recipes, page 185)
1 bay leaf
2 sprigs fresh thyme
1 pound string beans, trimmed
Salt and freshly ground pepper, to taste
3 cups steamed white rice, recipe follows

GARNISH
5 scallions, both white and green parts, chopped

STEAMED WHITE RICE
2 cups long grain rice
2 teaspoons salt
1 tablespoon unsalted butter

To make the steamed white rice: Combine the rice, 4 cups water, salt, and butter in a medium saucepan with a tight-fitting lid. Slowly bring to a boil over medium heat, stirring occasionally.

Cover and reduce the heat to low. Cook for 20 minutes, then remove from the heat and allow to stand an additional 10 minutes without removing the lid.

To make the Hoppin' John: Heat the oil in a large stock pot over medium heat. Add the lardons and cook for 5 minutes, until lightly browned.

Add the onion, celery, green pepper, and garlic, and cook 10 minutes, until soft. Stir in the drained black-eyed peas, stock, bay leaf, and thyme.

Bring to a boil, reduce the heat to low, and simmer for 30 minutes, stirring occasionally, until the peas are tender. Skim any foam off the top as necessary.

Add the string beans and cook an additional 10 minutes.

Before serving, fluff the rice with a fork. Stir the steamed rice into the pot of vegetables and adjust the seasonings with salt and pepper to taste.

Garnish with the green onions and serve hot or cold.

Rice Pilaf with *Beurre Noisette*

The Beurre Noisette, or browned butter, adds a sweet nuttiness to this dish.

Serves 6

4 cups Chicken Stock (recipe, page 185)
8 tablespoons butter
1 medium onion, finely diced (about 1 cup)
2 cups long grain rice
2 tablespoons fresh thyme leaves
1 bay leaf
Salt and freshly ground pepper, to taste

Preheat oven to 400°F.

In a medium saucepan over medium-high heat, bring the chicken stock to a boil.

In a large, oven-safe saucepan with a tight-fitting lid, brown the butter over medium-low heat 6 to 10 minutes, or until it stops foaming and turns a rich brown color. The browning butter should give off a nutty aroma.

Add the onions and rice and cook for 5 to 7 minutes, until the onion softens and the rice turns opaque.

Add the boiling stock, thyme, and bay leaf. Cover with the lid and bake in the preheated oven for 20 minutes.

Remove from the oven and allow to stand, without removing the lid, for 10 minutes.

Before serving, fluff the rice pilaf with a fork, and adjust the seasoning with salt and pepper.

VIDALIA ONION TART

Serves 6 to 8

1 Quick & Easy Tart Shell (recipe, page 182)

FILLING
**4 slices thick-cut hickory-smoked bacon, cut
into ¼-inch lardons**
2 tablespoons bacon grease
2 tablespoons unsalted butter
**1 pound yellow onions, halved from root to
stem, then thinly sliced crosswise (about 5
cups)**
**1 pound Vidalia onions, halved from root to
stem, then thinly sliced crosswise (about 5
cups)**
2 teaspoons sea salt
2 teaspoons freshly ground pepper
**2 cups Vidalia spring onions with the green
tops, cut on the bias**
½ cup crème fraîche
½ cup heavy cream
4 large eggs, room temperature
½ teaspoon freshly grated nutmeg

GARNISH
1 teaspoon fresh chopped thyme leaves
**½ cup Vidalia spring onions, green tops only,
cut on the bias**

Prepare the Tart Shell according to the recipe.

Cook the bacon lardons in a 12-inch cast-iron skillet over medium heat for 6 to 8 minutes, stirring occasionally, until crisp.

Using a slotted spoon, transfer the lardons to a paper towel-lined plate, and set aside.

Pour off the bacon grease, leaving about 2 tablespoons grease in the skillet. Add the butter and cook over medium heat until the butter stops foaming.

Add the yellow onions and Vidalia onions, the salt, and black pepper, and cook over low heat for 20 minutes, stirring occasionally, until the onions are very soft and light golden brown. (Do not over-brown the onions).

Stir in the Vidalia spring onions and lardons, and cook for an additional 5 minutes, then remove from the heat and set aside to cool.

In a large bowl, whisk together the crème fraîche, heavy cream, eggs, and nutmeg until well combined. Add the onion mixture and stir.

Pour the filling into the tart shell, spreading the onions out evenly, and bake for 25 to 30 minutes, until the filling is set and lightly browned. (The filling should have a slight jiggle when you gently shake the pan.)

Garnish with the fresh thyme leaves and Vidalia spring onion tops. Serve warm or at room temperature.

French Onion Soup

This iconic French soup proves that with a little imagination and the proper cooking technique, you can produce a delicious meal.

Serves 8

4 tablespoons olive oil
2 tablespoons butter
4 cups thinly sliced yellow onions
2 cups thinly sliced Vidalia onions
3 tablespoons flour
6 cups Beef Stock (recipe, page 184)
1 cup white wine
½ teaspoon sage
1 bay leaf
½ yellow onion, minced
3 tablespoons Cognac
½ cup grated Parmesan cheese
1½ cups grated Gruyere cheese
Salt and freshly ground pepper, to taste

CROUTONS
1 loaf French bread, cut into ½-inch slices
1 tablespoon olive oil

Heat the olive oil and butter in a large heavy stock pot over medium-low heat, until the butter stops foaming. Add the sliced onions, stirring until they are evenly coated.

Cover the stock pot with a tight fitting lid and cook for 20 minutes, until the onions are soft and tender.

Increase the heat to medium-high, add 1 teaspoon salt and continue cooking for 20 minutes, stirring occasionally, until the onions are browned.

Reduce the heat to medium-low and stir in the flour. Cook for 5 minutes, whisking constantly, until the flour forms a thick light brown paste (also called a roux).

Slowly whisk in 2 cups beef stock, whisking constantly. The stock and roux will make a thick sauce that will thin as you whisk in the remaining stock.

Add the remaining stock, wine, sage, and bay leaf.

Increase the heat to medium-high and bring to a boil, then reduce the heat to low and simmer, uncovered, whisking occasionally, for 30 minutes.

Preheat the oven to 325°F.

To make the croutons: Drizzle both sides of the French bread slices with olive oil, and place on a baking sheet. Bake for 10 minutes, then turn the slices and bake another 10 minutes.

When the soup has simmered for 30 minutes, remove from the heat and discard the bay leaf. Adjust the seasonings with salt and pepper to taste.

Stir in the Cognac, minced onion, and ½ cup grated Gruyere.

Ladle the soup into 8 heavy oven-proof soup crocks set on a baking sheet. Top each crock with the toasted bread, and top the bread with the Parmesan and remaining Gruyere cheese.

Bake for 30 minutes, until the cheese has melted. Turn the broiler on high and broil for 2 to 3 minutes until the cheese is golden brown.

Serve hot.

bell pepper

garlic

corn

celery

scallion

bacon

onion

tarragon

butter beans

fresh cream

purple hull peas

tomato

Succotash, page 57 and
Stewed tomatoes, Corn and Purple Hull Peas, page 56

★ ★ ★

SOUPS & STEWS

. . . .

*Potages &
Ragoûts*

⚜ ⚜ ⚜

STEWED TOMATOES, CORN, & PURPLE HULL PEAS

Serves 6 to 8

2 tablespoons olive oil
1 large onion, diced
3 large clove garlic, minced
1½ pounds tomatoes, diced (about 3 cups)
1 pound fresh purple hull peas, or dried peas
   that are soaked overnight in enough water
   to cover
2 cups Vegetable Stock (recipe, page 185)
   + more as needed
2 cups fresh corn kernels
Salt and freshly ground pepper, to taste

Heat the olive oil in a medium stockpot over medium-low heat. Add the onion, garlic, and diced tomatoes and cook for 15 minutes, stirring occasionally, until the onions are soft and any liquid from the tomatoes has cooked off.

Add the peas and stock to the tomato mixture (2 cups stock for fresh peas, or 5 cups stock for dried peas) and cook, covered, for 25 to 35 minutes, until the peas are tender. Add additional stock as needed.

Remove the lid, add the corn kernels, and season with salt and pepper to taste.

Serve warm.

PURPLE HULL PEAS

As kids, my sisters, cousins, and I would always help with chores around the farm. One summer my grandfather brought home 3 huge sacks full of purple hull peas. He told us he'd give us each a quarter to shell them. After about an hour of work-and no visible headway, we asked for a raise. When my grandfather said no, we went on strike, marching around the front yard with our handmade signs. He thought that was the funniest thing he'd ever seen and gave us each a dollar-after he finished drying his eyes from laughing so hard.

Succotash with Tarragon and Crème Fraiche

My version of Succotash adds a French accent, with a pinch of tarragon and a l ittle crème fraiche.

Serves 6 to 8

2 teaspoons salt
2 cups butter beans, fresh or frozen
1 tablespoon unsalted butter
6 strips thick-cut hickory-smoked bacon,
    cut into ¼-inch lardons
1 small sweet onion, finely diced
3 celery ribs, ¼-inch dice
1 medium red bell pepper, stemmed, seeded
    and cut into ¼-inch dice
2 cups corn kernels, fresh or frozen
2 large cloves garlic, minced
4 scallions, white and green parts, finely diced
1 cup heavy cream
2 tablespoons fresh tarragon, coarsely chopped
Salt and freshly ground pepper, to taste

GARNISH
¼ cup crème fraiche
1 teaspoon fresh chopped tarragon leaves

Bring 1 quart salted water to a rolling boil over medium-high heat. Add the butter beans and cook for 3 to 5 minutes for fresh beans and 5 to 10 minutes if using frozen beans.

Remove from the heat, drain and set aside.

Melt the butter in a large sauté pan over medium heat. Add the lardons and cook for 7 minutes, or until crisp. Stir in the onion, celery, and bell pepper, stirring to coat with the butter and bacon fat. Cook 5 minutes, until tender.

Add the corn, garlic, and scallions, and cook an additional 5 minutes, stirring occasionally.

Add the cooked butter beans to the pan and stir to combine.

Stir in the heavy cream and tarragon.

Reduce the heat to low, and cook uncovered for 5 more minutes, or until the succotash is heated through.

Season liberally with salt and black pepper, and garnish each serving with the crème fraiche and tarragon.

BRAISED PIG FEET *with Hot Peppers*

I was surprised to learn that pig feet are as popular in France as they are in the South. Imagine my surpise!

Serves 8

8 large pig feet, quartered
2 large onions, diced
3 large cloves garlic, mashed
1 tablespoon sea salt
1 teaspoon freshly ground black pepper
1 tablespoon Pickling Spice (recipe, page 189)
3 bay leaves
½ cup cider vinegar
6 to 8 dried chili peppers, or 1 tablespoon
   dried red pepper flakes
1 quart Vegetable Stock (recipe, page 185) +
   more as needed
3 large ripe tomatoes, diced (about 3 cups)
¼ cup firmly packed brown sugar
4 cups cooked white rice (recipe,
   page 50, or cook according to package
   directions)

GARNISH
¼ cup flatleaf parsley, chopped

Wash the pig feet in cold water until the water runs clear.

Place in a large stock pot and add the onions, garlic, sea salt, pepper, pickling spice, bay leaves, vinegar, and chili peppers. Cover with the vegetable stock and stir.

Bring to a boil over high heat, then reduce the heat to low and simmer for 3 hours, until tender. Skim off any foam as needed. Add additional stock to keep the pig feet covered in liquid during the cooking time.

When the pig feet are tender, add the diced tomatoes and sugar, adjust the seasoning with salt and pepper, and simmer for an additional 1 hour, until the sauce is thick and gelatinous.

Prepare the white rice according to directions.

Serve over hot white rice and garnish with chopped parsley. Add a side of Red Pepper Sauce (recipe, page 18).

pig feet

bay leaves

dried spices

onion

garlic

rice

black and yellow
mustard seeds

brown sugar

cayenne peppers

Braised Pig Feet with Hot Peppers, page 58 and
Roasted Pig Feet with Whole Grain Mustard, page 61

Roasted Pig Feet with Whole Grain Mustard

Serves 8

8 pig feet, split in half
2 large onions, peeled and quartered
1 head garlic, cut crossways
1 bay leaf
½ cup cider vinegar
1 dried cayenne pepper
1 tablespoon sea salt
1teaspoon freshly cracked black pepper
1 quart Vegetable Stock (recipe, page 185)
1 large onion, diced
3 large cloves garlic, smashed
Salt and black pepper, to taste

GARNISH
Whole Grain Mustard (recipe, page 190)

Wash the pig feet in cold water until the water runs clear. Place in a large stock pot and add the onions, garlic, bay leaf, vinegar, cayenne pepper, salt, and pepper. Cover with the vegetable stock and bring to a boil over medium-high heat, then reduce the heat to low and simmer for 2 hours, until tender. Do not overcook, as you want the pig feet to remain whole. Add additional stock as needed to keep the pig feet covered during the cooking time.

Preheat the oven to 400°F

When tender, transfer the pig feet to a large roasting pan, and place them skin-side up. Strain the cooking liquid, discarding the solids, and reserve.

Add 2 cups reserved cooking liquid, the diced onion, and smashed garlic to the roasting pan with the pig feet, and sprinkle liberally with salt and black pepper, to taste. Discard the remaining cooking liquid.

Roast for 30 minutes, occasionally basting the pig feet with the cooking liquid from the roasting pan until the skin is brown and crispy. Serve with the sauce from the roasting pan and pass the Whole Grain Mustard.

LOVELY AWFUL OFFAL

My love of castoff pieces and feet began at an early age.

When I was dating the boy I would later marry, I brought him home to meet my grandmother. The first childhood story she told him was how much I loved chicken feet as a young girl. Her words, to be exact, were, "Jenny loved eating fried chicken feet when she was little." I. Was. Mortified.

Didn't my Gram sense that I was trying to marry this boy? Couldn't she tell he wasn't "country?" In retrospect, she did know, and she could see. She was just making sure that he knew that when we did marry, I would always be that little girl who loved fried chicken feet.

And I still do… and livers, gizzards, pig feet, and lamb shanks. I'm crazy about chitterlings and tripe and—although frowned upon by many—I'm a sucker for the gristle on the joint end of a smoked ham hock. So, although all those pieces and parts are often dismissed and called "awful offal," I think they're just lovely.

CRAB, SHRIMP & OYSTER GUMBO

Everyone has their favorite version of gumbo, so don't be shy about making this dish your own by adding cooked chicken, sausage, or even okra before serving.

Serves 8

¼ cup vegetable oil
1 small onion, diced (about ½ cup)
2 celery stalks, diced (about ½ cup)
1 green bell pepper, diced (about 1 cup)
¼ cup all-purpose flour
1 ripe tomato, diced (about ½ cup)
4 large cloves garlic, minced
2 quarts Fish or Shrimp Stock (recipes, pages 186 and 187)
8 blue claw crabs, cut in half-lengthwise
6 bay leaves
1 teaspoon dried oregano
1 teaspoon dried thyme leaves
3 tablespoons file powder
1 tablespoon salt
1 teaspoon freshly ground pepper
1 teaspoon cayenne
4 cups cooked long-grain white rice (recipe, page 50), or cook according to the package directions)
1 pound Gulf shrimp, peeled and deveined
2 cups shucked fresh oysters, with their liquid
¼ cup chopped green onions

Add the oil to a large stock pot over medium-high heat. When the oil is hot, add the onions, celery, and green peppers and sauté for 1 minute.

Reduce the heat to low and stir in the flour. Cook for 7 minutes, stirring constantly, until flour turns a dark brown.

Stir in the diced tomatoes and garlic, and cook for an additional 15 minutes.

Pour the fish or shrimp stock into the flour mixture in a steady stream, whisking constantly, and simmer for 30 minutes until the stock thickens. Add the crab claws, bay leaves, oregano, and thyme.

Increase the heat to high, bring to a boil, and cook for 10 minutes.

Stir the file powder into 1 cup cold water until it dissolves, and whisk this directly into the stockpot. Season with cayenne, salt, and pepper to taste.

Reduce the temperature to low and simmer for 15 minutes, skimming any foam from the top of the gumbo.

While the gumbo is simmering, prepare the rice.

After 15 minutes, increase the heat to high and bring the gumbo back up to a boil. Add the shrimp and oysters to the boiling gumbo all at once, then reduce the heat to low and simmer for a final 5 minutes.

Remove from the heat and serve over the hot rice. Garnish with the chopped green onions.

Bouillabaisse

What makes a bouillabaisse different from other fish soups is the selection of Provençal herbs and spices and the method of serving. Tradionally, the broth is served first in a soup plate with slices of bread and rouille, then the fish is served separately on a large platter. I like to serve it more simply, as Julia Child suggests: the fish and broth are brought to the table separately and served together in large soup plates.

Serves 8

ROUILLE
2 large egg yolks
1 tablespoon Dijon mustard
2 cloves garlic
¼ teaspoon saffron threads
¼ teaspoon cayenne
¼ teaspoon paprika
1 cup olive oil
½ cup fresh bread crumbs
Sea salt and freshly ground pepper, to taste

CROUTONS
16 (½-inch thick) baguette slices, cut on
  the bias
1 large clove garlic, peeled
2 tablespoons olive oil
Sea salt and freshly ground pepper

BOUILLABAISSE
3 tablespoons extra-virgin olive oil + morc for
  drizzling
2 leeks, both white and light green parts,
  thinly sliced
1 large onion, diced (about 1 cup)
1 fennel bulb, diced (about ½ cup)
4 cloves garlic, coarsely chopped
2 large ripe tomatoes, diced (about 2 cups)
2 bay leaves
¼ teaspoon saffron threads

2 tablespoons pastis, or Pernod
6 cups Fish Stock (recipe, page 186)
3 Yukon Gold potatoes (about 1½ pounds),
  peeled and diced
¼ teaspoon cayenne
Sea salt and freshly ground pepper, to taste
2 dozen littleneck clams, scrubbed
1 pound monkfish, cut into 2-inch pieces
1 pound skinless red snapper fillets, cut into
  2-inch pieces
1 pound skinless halibut or sea bass fillets,
  cut into 2-inch pieces

To make the Rouille: In a food processor, combine the egg yolks, mustard, garlic, saffron, cayenne, and paprika and pulse until well combined. With the machine running, drizzle in the olive oil and process until the Rouille is smooth.

Transfer to a bowl and stir in enough bread crumbs to thicken the rouille into a paste. Season with salt and pepper, cover, and refrigerate.

To make the Croutons: Preheat the broiler to high. Arrange the baguette slices on a baking sheet and broil for 1 minute per side, until golden brown. Remove from the oven and rub each slice with the garlic clove, drizzle lightly with the olive oil, and sprinkle liberally with salt and pepper.

To make the Bouillabaisse: Heat the olive oil in a large stock pot over medium-low heat. Add the leeks, onion, fennel, and chopped garlic, and cook 5 minutes, until the onions and leeks are soft. Add the tomatoes and cook for 5 minutes, until they begin to soften.

Add the bay leaves, saffron, and pastis and bring to a boil.

Add the fish stock and reduce the heat to a simmer. Cook for 20 minutes, until the vegetables are very tender. Remove and discard the bay leaves.

Using a hand blender, pulse the vegetables and broth to a smooth puree. (If you use a food processor, work in batches.) Strain the puree through a fine sieve set over a very large stock pot; discard any solids.

Add the potatoes and cayenne pepper to the stock pot with the puree, and simmer on low heat for 10 minutes, until the potatoes are just tender; season with salt and pepper.

Add the clams, cover the stock pot, and cook for 3 minutes until the clams just begin to open. Add the monkfish, cover, and simmer for an additional 2 minutes. Add the snapper and halibut, cover and simmer another 4 minutes, until the clams are fully open and the fish is cooked through.

To plate: Set a crouton spread with rouille in each of 8 shallow bowls and ladle the fish and broth on top, drizzle with olive oil.

Serve the additional rouille and croutons on the side.

PINTO BEANS & SMOKED HAM HOCKS

Serves 4 to 6

1 pound dry pinto beans, rinsed and soaked overnight in enough cold water to cover
8 cups Vegetable Stock + more as needed
1 large smoked ham hock
1 large onion, diced (about 1½ cups)
2 cloves garlic, smashed
1 cayenne pepper
Salt and freshly ground pepper, to taste

Discard the soaking liquid and add the beans, stock, ham hock, onion, garlic, and cayenne pepper to a large stockpot. Bring to a boil over medium-high heat, then reduce the heat to medium-low, and simmer for at least 4 hours, or until the beans are soft. Add additional stock as needed. The longer you simmer the pinto beans, the thicker the broth will become.

Remove the ham hock from the broth, and set aside to cool. Remove the meat and skin from the bone. Dice the meat and skin and return them to the stockpot, discarding the bone. Adjust the seasonings with salt and pepper to taste.

Cassoulet

Serves 8

2 smoked ham hocks

1 pound boneless pork shoulder, cut into
    1½-inch cubes

Salt and freshly ground pepper, to taste

2 pounds dried pinto beans, rinsed

8 ounces salt pork, with skin attached

1 pound smoked Andouille sausage, cut into
    4-inch pieces

1 carrot, unpeeled, cut into 3-inch sections

1 medium onion, quartered

1 whole head garlic, cut in half crosswise

1 large tomato, diced

1 bouquet garni (recipe below)

2 quarts + 2 cups Chicken Stock (recipe, page 185)

6 duck confit legs (recipe, page 133)

1 tablespoon olive oil

¼ cup fresh bread crumbs

BOUQUET GARNI

4 sprigs parsley

3 small celery stalks

2 sprigs thyme

1 bay leaf

6 whole cloves

Place the ham hocks and pork shoulder cubes in a medium bowl and season lightly with salt and pepper; cover and refrigerate overnight.

In a separate large bowl, cover the dried beans with at least 3 inches water and soak overnight.

The next day, in a medium saucepan over medium-high heat, add enough water to cover the salt pork by 2 inches and bring to a boil. Reduce the heat to a simmer and cook for 30 minutes, until the salt pork is supple. Drain, cool and set the salt pork aside.

Drain the beans, rinse, and set them aside.

In a large, heavy-bottom Dutch oven, heat the duck fat over medium-high heat.

Add half the seasoned pork cubes and cook 10 minutes, until lightly browned; transfer to a plate. Repeat with the remaining pork cubes and set aside. Add the ham hocks to the Dutch oven and brown them lightly.

Add the Andouille sausage, carrots, and onions to the pot and cook over medium heat for 7 minutes, stirring occasionally, until the onions are golden. Add the cut head of garlic and the diced tomato, and cook for 1 minute, stirring constantly.

To make the Bouquet Garni: Gather the ingredients together in a piece of cheesecloth, and tie with butcher's twine.

Pour in 2 quarts chicken stock to the pot and add the bouquet garni, cloves, boiled salt pork, the browned pork cubes, and the beans. Bring to a boil over high heat, then cover the pot with a tight-fitting lid, and reduce the heat to medium-low. Simmer for 2 hours, stirring occasionally.

Remove from the heat and discard the cut garlic and bouquet garni.

Preheat the oven to 325°F.

Add the remaining 2 cups chicken stock to the Dutch oven, and season with salt and pepper. Place the duck confit in an even layer on top of the cassoulet, skin side up. Bake the cassoulet, uncovered, for 1½ hours.

Reduce the temperature to 275°F. Gently stir the skin that has formed atop the cassoulet. Sprinkle with the bread crumbs, and bake for 1 additional hour, uncovered, until a rich brown crust has formed on the surface.

Remove from the oven and let rest for at least 20 to 30 minutes before serving.

SUMMER VEGETABLE SOUP *with Tomato Relish*

One of the advantages of soups like Summer Vegetable Soup and Soupe au Pistou is that you can use whatever vegetables are in season. For added variety, use different types of dried beans, pasta, or even rice.

Serves 8

4 tablespoons olive oil
2 large onions, diced (about 2 cups)
2 tablespoons garlic, finely minced
2 large celery stalks, diced (about ½ cups)
Kosher salt
2 medium carrots, peeled and cut into rounds
2 medium zucchini, diced (about 2 cups)
**3 medium Yukon Gold potatoes, peeled and
    diced (about 2 cups)**
**1 pound fresh green beans, trimmed and cut
    into ¾-inch pieces (about 2 cups)**
**2 quarts Chicken or Vegetable Stock (recipes,
    page 185)**
**6 large ripe tomatoes, peeled, seeded, and
    diced (about 2 cups)**
Kernels from 2 ears corn (about 2 cups)
½ teaspoon freshly ground pepper
**¼ cup fresh flatleaf parsley leaves, chopped,
    and firmly packed**

GARNISH
½ cup Tomato Relish, (recipe, page 16)

Heat the olive oil in a large, heavy-bottomed stockpot or Dutch oven over medium-low heat.

Add the onion, garlic, celery, and a pinch of salt, and cook for 7 to 8 minutes, until the vegetables begin to soften.

Add the carrots, zucchini, potatoes, and green beans and cook an additional 5 minutes, stirring occasionally.

Add the stock, increase the heat to high, and bring to a simmer. Once simmering, add the tomatoes, corn, and black pepper.

Reduce the heat to low, cover, and simmer for 20 minutes, until the vegetables are fork tender.

Remove from the heat and add the parsley. Season to taste with salt and pepper.

Garnish each serving with Tomato Relish and serve immediately.

Soupe au Pistou

Serves 8

1 cup dried kidney beans, covered with at least
   2 inches cold water, and soaked overnight
1 cup dried cannellini beans, covered with at
   least 2 inches cold water, and soaked overnight
2 bay leaves
3 tablespoons olive oil
2 medium onions, peeled and diced (about
   1½ cups)
1 leek, white and light green parts only, thinly
   sliced (about 1 cup)
2 teaspoons chopped fresh thyme
2 medium carrots, peeled and diced
2 medium zucchini, diced (about 2 cups)
½ pound green beans, tips removed and
   cut crosswise into quarters (about 2 cups)
6 cloves garlic, thinly sliced
4 large ripe tomatoes, seeded and diced
   (about 3 cups)
1 tablespoon sea salt
Freshly ground pepper, to taste
1 cup dried small pasta, such as orzo, or elbow

PISTOU
1 large clove garlic, peeled
Pinch of salt
2 cups fresh basil leaves, firmly packed
¼ cup olive oil
1 tomato, peeled, seeded and diced (¼ cup)
2 tablespoons grated Parmesan cheese

GARNISH
¼ cup grated Parmesan cheese
Olive oil

To make the Pistou: Using a small food processor, pulse the garlic and salt until coarsely chopped.

Add the basil leaves, tomato and cheese to the garlic and pulse until well combined.

Drizzle in the olive oil and pulse until smooth. Adjust to taste with additional salt, and set aside.

To make the Soupe: Add the soaked and drained beans, bay leaves, and 6 cups water to a large saucepan over medium-high heat. Bring to a boil, and cook the beans for 1 hour, until just tender, adding more water as necessary to keep the beans covered. Be careful not to overcook.

Once cooked, remove from the stove and set aside. Discard the bay leaves.

In a large stockpot, heat the olive oil over medium heat. Add the onions and leeks and cook, stirring occasionally, until soft and translucent; about 5 minutes.

Add the thyme, diced carrots, zucchini, green beans, garlic, and tomatoes. Season with salt and pepper to taste.

Cook for 10 minutes, stirring occasionally, until the vegetables are completely tender.

Add the cooked beans with their cooking liquid to the vegetables, plus 6 to 8 cups water. Increase the heat to high and bring the soup to a boil.

Add the pasta and boil for 7 minutes, until the pasta is tender but still firm.

To serve, ladle the hot soup into bowls and top with a generous spoonful of pistou. Garnish with a sprinkle of Parmesan and a drizzle of olive oil.

chives

celery

garlic

shallots

rice

shrimp

lemons

parsley

pickling spice

Pickled Shrimp & Onions, page 74, and **Shrimp Creole,** page 76

★★★

FISH & SEAFOOD

∙∙∙∙∙∙∙∙∙∙∙∙∙∙∙∙∙∙∙∙∙∙∙∙∙∙∙∙∙∙∙∙∙∙∙∙∙∙

Poissons &
Fruits de Mer

⚜ ⚜ ⚜

butter

blue crabs

lemongrass

lemon

cayenne

chiles

artichoke

grated Parmesan

chives

milk

Blue Crab & Artichoke Dip, page 72 and
Artichoke & Crab Soufflé, page 73

HOW TO EAT BLUE CRABS

1.

Turn the steamed or boiled crab over so that its belly
faces you. Using your fingers, lift up its tail, and pull it back to
snap it off of the body.

2.

Using a butter knife, remove the top shell from the bottom of the body,
by twisting and prying it away with the butter knife. Discard the shell.

3.

Remove the gills, often called "dead man's fingers," which are attached
to either side of the crab. Don't panic when you see the yellowish
"mustard" and perhaps the orange roe (eggs)—both are edible.
Crack the body down the center.

4.

Press lightly on the body where the back legs—or "swimmers"—are
attached, and pull out the backfin meat in the rear of the crab.
Using your fingers, remove the remaining body meat.

5.

Remove the claws and use a crab cracker, or a small
wooden mallet, to gently crack open the claws. Scrape
the meat out of the claws with your fingers
or a butter knife.

BLUE CRAB & ARTICHOKE DIP

Serves 6

2 tablespoons butter, room temperature
1 pound cream cheese, room temperature
⅔ cup shredded sharp cheddar cheese
   + 2 tablespoons for topping
½ cup finely diced red bell pepper
⅓ cup chopped green onions
½ cup sour cream
¼ cup mayonnaise (recipe, page 183)
3 large cloves garlic, minced
Zest and juice of 1 lemon
2 teaspoons chopped fresh tarragon
1 teaspoon Worcestershire sauce
1 pinch cayenne pepper
1 pound Blue Crab crabmeat, picked
2 cups chopped artichoke bottoms
Salt and freshly ground pepper, to taste

Preheat the oven to 375°F.

Butter a deep 8x8-inch baking dish.

In a large bowl, combine the cream cheese, cheddar cheese, red bell pepper, green onions, sour cream, mayonnaise, garlic, lemon zest and juice, tarragon, Worcestershire sauce, and the cayenne pepper and mix well.

Stir in the crabmeat and artichoke bottoms; adjust the seasoning with salt and black pepper.

Spread into the buttered baking dish and top with 2 tablespoons cheddar cheese

Bake in the preheated oven for 30 minutes, or until the dip is bubbling hot and golden brown on top.

Serve hot.

Artichoke & Crab Soufflé

The first time I baked a soufflé, I made everyone in the house sit very still and whisper—if they had to talk at all! But the reality is that the success of this infamous egg dish is about whipping in lots of air, baking in a hot, hot oven, and serving it as soon as possible. Tip-toeing around the kitchen won't help.

Serves 6

2 tablespoons unsalted butter, room temperature
¾ cup + 2 tablespoons grated Parmesan cheese, divided
6 large egg yolks
1 teaspoon salt
¾ cup coarsely chopped artichoke hearts
¾ cup lump crabmeat
2 tablespoons fresh whole tarragon leaves
¼ cup butter
5 tablespoons all-purpose flour
1 large shallot, minced
1 pinch cayenne pepper
1¼ cups whole milk
¼ cup dry white wine
2 tablespoons hot sauce
8 large egg whites

Position the oven rack to the center of the oven and preheat to 400°F.

Butter six (1¼-cup) soufflé cups with 2 tablespoons butter and sprinkle with 2 tablespoons grated Parmesan cheese to coat.

Place on a rimmed baking sheet and set aside.

Whisk the egg yolks and salt together in a small bowl and set aside.

In a separate bowl, combine the chopped artichoke hearts, crabmeat, and tarragon and set aside.

Melt ¼ cup butter in a large, heavy-bottom saucepan over medium heat. Add the flour, shallot and cayenne and whisk constantly for 3 minutes, or until the mixture bubbles but does not brown.

Gradually whisk in the milk, then the wine, whisking constantly for 2 minutes until the sauce is smooth and thick. Remove from the heat.

In a little bowl, mix together 2 tablespoons hot sauce to the egg yolk mixture. This will temper the egg yolks and prevent them from "scrambling" in the hot sauce.

Add the tempered yolk mixture to the hot sauce all at once; whisking to combine. Stir in the artichoke and crab mixture and set aside.

In a large bowl, use a whisk or whip attachment of an electric mixer to beat the egg whites until stiff, but not dry.

Fold ¼ of the beaten egg whites into the lukewarm egg, crab, and artichoke mixture. Fold in ¾ cup Parmesan cheese and the remaining whites.

Transfer the soufflé mixture to the prepared soufflé cups.

Place in the preheated oven and bake for 20 minutes, until the soufflé has doubled in size and is light golden brown.

Remove the soufflés from the oven and serve immediately.

PICKLED SHRIMP & ONIONS

I didn't taste pickled shrimp until I moved to Georgia, but it was love at first taste.

Serves 8

1 cup extra virgin olive oil
2/3 cups apple cider vinegar
1/3 cup water
1 large lemon, sliced
1/2 cup flatleaf parsley leaves, firmly packed
2 tablespoons kosher salt
1 teaspoon red pepper flakes
4 large cloves garlic, peeled and sliced
1/2 cup Shrimp & Crab Pickling Spice
  (recipe, page 188)
2 pounds large shrimp, peeled and deveined
6 dried cayenne peppers
12 dried bay leaves
1 large yellow onion, thinly sliced
  lengthwise

In a large bowl, combine the oil, vinegar, 1/3 cup water, sliced lemon, parsley leaves, salt, red pepper, and garlic together, and set aside.

Add the Shrimp & Crab Pickling Spice and 2 quarts water to a large stock pot over medium-high heat and bring to a rolling boil. Add the shrimp and cook for 3 minutes, until tthey are bright pink. Drain and set aside.

Layer the hot shrimp, dried cayenne peppers, bay leaves and sliced onions in a 2-quart glass jar. Pour in the oil and vinegar mixture, making sure all of the shrimp and onions are covered.

Cover the jar a lid, or with plastic wrap, and refrigerate for at least 24 hours before serving. The Pickled Shrimp & Onions taste better the longer they sit, and will keep refrigerated for up to 1 week.

Shrimp Creole

Serves 6

2½ pounds large shrimp, peeled, tail
    removed, and deveined
1 tablespoon Southern Seasoning Salt (recipe,
    page 188)
2 tablespoons all-purpose flour
1 cup shrimp or Fish Stock (recipe, page 186)
4 ounces (1 stick) butter
2 large onions, diced (about 2 cups)
1 large green bell pepper, diced (about 1 cup)
5 celery stalks, diced (about 1 cup)
3 large cloves garlic, minced (about
    1 tablespoon)
Salt and freshly ground pepper, to taste
¼ teaspoon cayenne pepper
2 bay leaves
2 pounds tomatoes (about 4 cups) peeled,
    seeded and chopped
1 teaspoon Worcestershire Sauce
1 teaspoon hot sauce
6 scallions, chopped (about ½ cup)
2 tablespoons fresh flatleaf parsley, chopped
4 cups cooked long-grain white rice

Season the shrimp with Southern Seasoning Salt and set aside.

In a separate bowl, whisk the flour and stock together and set aside.

Melt the butter in a large 4-quart saucepan over medium-low heat. Add the onions, peppers, celery, and garlic. Season with salt, black pepper, and cayenne pepper and cook for 6 to 8 minutes, until soft.

Stir in the bay leaves and diced tomatoes

Increase the heat to medium-high, bring to a boil, then reduce the heat to low and simmer for 15 minutes.

Stir in the Worcestershire sauce and hot sauce.

Whisk the flour mixture into the saucepan and continue to simmer for 4 to 6 minutes.

Add the seasoned shrimp to the mixture and continue cooking for 4 minutes, until the shrimp turn bright pink. Remove from the heat.

Stir in the scallions and parsley.

Adjust the seasoning with salt and cayenne pepper, as needed.

Prepare the rice according to the package directions. Serve the Shrimp Creole over the rice.

PAN-SEARED TROUT

Fresh herbs, tart lemon, and rich butter dress up this ordinary fish, making it a simple and delicious weeknight meal.

Serves 6

6 tablespoons vegetable oil, divided
1½ cups fresh, unseasoned breadcrumbs
¼ cup fresh flatleaf parsley, chopped
1 tablespoon fresh lemon zest
Salt and freshly ground pepper
6 (8-ounce) trout fillets, skin on

GARNISH
1 lemon, cut into 6 wedges
¼ cup unsalted butter, melted
1 tablespoon fresh flatleaf parsley, chopped

Preheat the oven to 300°F.

Mix together the breadcrumbs, parsley, lemon zest and 1 teaspoon salt and pepper and place on a baking sheet. Set aside.

Liberally season all 6 trout fillets with salt and pepper. Hold each fillet flesh side down and press it firmly into the breadcrumb mixture to coat.

Heat 3 tablespoons oil in a large cast-iron skillet over medium-high heat. Cook 3 trout fillets, starting with the breadcrumb-side down, and cook 3 minutes then turn and cook an additional 3 minutes, until the skin is crisp and golden brown. Transfer the fish, breaded-side-up, to a clean baking sheet and place in the preheated oven to keep warm while you continue cooking the remaining trout.

Repeat the process, using the remaining oil and fillets.

Remove the trout from the oven and place on a warm platter. Drizzle with melted butter and garnish with lemon wedges and fresh parsley.

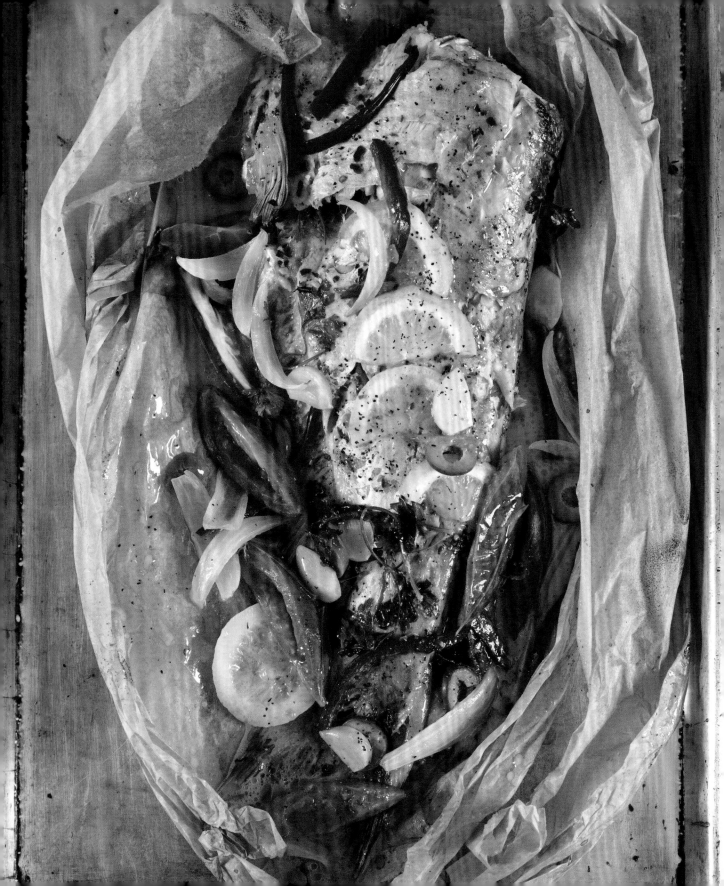

Poisson au Papillote

"En Papillote" is the French method of wrapping raw ingredients in a parcel of parchment paper and roasting in a hot oven, allowing steam to build to cook the food. Always open your parchment parcel in front of your dinner guests for a dramatic reveal.

Serves 6

2 sheets parchment paper, each about
  16 inches long
1 whole fish (about 2 pounds), cleaned
  and scaled,
Salt and freshly ground pepper, to taste
½ cup olive oil
¼ cup fresh flatleaf parsley, coarsely chopped,
  plus 3 sprigs
6 large cloves garlic, thinly sliced
¼ teaspoon red pepper flakes
4 large Roma tomatoes, quartered
1 large red bell pepper, cut into strips
1 large lemon, sliced, + 1 small lemon, cut
  into 8 wedges
8 fresh sprigs thyme
½ cup Spanish olives with pimentos
⅓ cup dry white wine

Heat the oven to 450°F.

Liberally season the fish, inside and out, with salt and pepper and set aside on a platter.

In a bowl, combine the oil, chopped parsley, garlic, and red pepper flakes, and set aside.

Place a sheet of parchment paper on a large baking sheet and add half the oil mixture in the center of the paper as a bed for the fish.

Place half the tomatoes, bell pepper, sliced lemon, thyme, and olives on the oil mixture. Place the fish on top.

Tuck the parsley sprigs and lemon wedges inside the fish. Pour the remaining oil on top of the fish and add the remaining tomatoes, bell pepper, sliced lemon, thyme and olives. Season with salt and pepper.

Top with the thyme, and pour the wine over the fish.

To seal the papillote, cover the entire fish with the second sheet of parchment paper and, starting at one end, fold both pieces of parchment paper together along the outside edge; in tight overlapping folds. Tuck the last fold under the papillote.

Place the baking sheet in the preheated oven and roast for 20 to 25 minutes. The parchment paper will rise as the steam builds inside the papillote.

Transfer the papillote to a warm platter, carefully slit the top of the paper with a sharp knife and serve immediately.

See Making en Papillot, page 80.

Making en Papillote

1. Gather mise en picae.

2. Place on a parchment-lined pan.

3. Fill the fish with fresh herbs.

7. Drizzle with olive oil.

8. Cover with parchment paper.

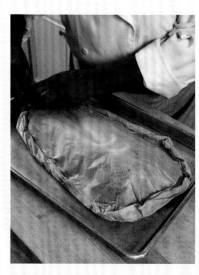
9. Fold the edges tightly.

4. Season liberally.

5. Tuck the fish over the herbs.

6. Add the remaining ingredients.

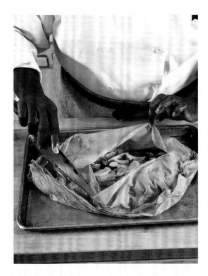

10. Remove from the the oven and slice open.

11. Baste with the juices.

12. Serve on the parchment-lined pan.

SEARED SALMON FILLETS
with Fresh Herb Sauce

In addition to salmon, you can use any fatty fish, such as catfish or sea bass for this recipe.

Serves 6

FRESH HERB SAUCE
3 scallions, white and green parts, chopped
¼ cup fresh basil leaves, loosely packed
¼ cup fresh flatleaf parsley leaves, tightly
   packed
1 tablespoon freshly squeezed lemon juice
2 teaspoons Dijon mustard
1½ teaspoons olive oil
2 cloves garlic
1 teaspoon kosher salt
½ teaspoon freshly ground pepper
½ cup mayonnaise (recipe, page 183)
¼ cup plain Greek yogurt
¼ cup buttermilk

FILLETS
6 (6-ounce) salmon fillets
Kosher salt and freshly ground pepper
¼ cup good quality olive oil
2 tablespoons freshly squeezed lemon juice

Place all of the ingredients for the Fresh Herb Sauce in a blender, or a small food processor fitted with a blade attachment, and pulse until smooth. Adjust the seasoning with salt and pepper.

Transfer to a small bowl, cover, and refrigerate for at least 1 hour. The sauce will thicken as it chills.

Place the salmon fillets in a glass baking dish and season generously with kosher salt and pepper.

In a small bowl, whisk together the olive oil and lemon juice, and pour evenly over the salmon. Let it sit at room temperature for 15 minutes.

Heat a large, heavy sauté pan on high heat, then reduce the heat to medium and add the salmon, skin-side down, in the pan. Cook for 8 to 10 minutes. Do not turn. The salmon is done when it flakes easily with a fork.

Transfer the salmon to a platter and serve with the Fresh Herb Sauce.

Salmon Croquettes with Remoulade Sauce

Serves 8

**2 pounds cooked salmon, or 2 pounds
    uncooked salmon fillets**
**1 medium onion, finely chopped (about
    ½ cups)**
4 large eggs, room temperature
½ cup fresh bread crumbs
½ cup flour
¼ cup yellow cornmeal
Salt and freshly ground pepper, to taste
½ teaspoon paprika
1 teaspoon lemon zest
¼ cup fresh flatleaf parsley, chopped
½ cup vegetable oil, for frying
Remoulade Sauce (recipe, page 183)

To cook the salmon: Heat a large, heavy sauté pan over high heat. Rub the salmon with vegetable oil and place it, skin-side down, in the pan to cook for 3 minutes. Decrease the heat to medium, and cook for an additional 5 minutes. Do not turn. The salmon is done when it flakes easily with a fork.

Break the salmon into small pieces and add them to a large bowl. Add the onion, eggs, breadcrumbs, flour, cornmeal, salt, pepper, paprika, and lemon zest and stir until well incorporated.

Use your hands to form the salmon mixture into 8 croquettes, place on a platter, and refrigerate for at least 30 minutes, or overnight. It doesn't matter what size you make your croquettes, so long as they are all the same size; to ensure even cooking.

Heat the vegetable oil in a large skillet over medium-high heat until a probe thermometer reads 350° to 375°F.

Remove the salmon croquettes from the refrigerator and add them one at a time to the hot oil. Do not crowd; you may want to cook them in two batches. Cook 5 minutes on each side, until they are golden brown.

Remove and drain on a paper-towel-lined platter.

Serve hot with the Remoulade Sauce.

PECAN-CRUSTED CATFISH FILLETS

Serves 6

6 (6-ounce) catfish fillets
1 tablespoon salt
2 tablespoons freshly ground pepper
1 cup milk
2 large eggs
1 cup cornmeal
¾ cup coarsely chopped pecans
⅓ cup flour
Vegetable oil, for frying

Season the catfish liberally with salt and pepper and set aside.

In a small bowl, whisk together the milk and eggs, then pour into an 8x8-inch baking dish. Set aside.

Place the cornmeal, pecans, 1 tablespoon salt, and 2 teaspoons pepper in the bowl of a food processor, using the blade attachment, and pulse until the mixture resembles coarse breadcrumbs.

Pour the cornmeal mixture onto a plate.

Pour the flour onto a separate plate.

Heat 2 inches of the vegetable oil in a large Dutch oven over medium-high heat until a probe thermometer reads 350° to 375°F.

Dip the fish into the flour, then into the egg mixture, and finally into the cornmeal mixture, being sure to completely coat each catfish fillet.

Fry the pecan-crusted catfish for 5 minutes on each side, until golden brown.

Serve with Red Pepper Sauce (recipe, page 18), or Remoulade Sauce (recipe, page 183).

Blackened Catfish with Beurre Blanc Sauce

Beurre Blanc, or "white butter," is made by blending a reduction of white wine and shallots with cold butter, resulting in a smooth, silky sauce. The key to successfully making this sauce is to stir in the initial cubes of cold butter while the pan is off the heat.

Serves 6

¼ cup vegetable oil, for frying
6 catfish fillets
¼ cup Blackening Spice (recipe, page 189)

BEURRE BLANC SAUCE
¼ cup dry white wine
¼ cup white wine vinegar
1 tablespoon minced shallots
¼ teaspoon kosher salt
Pinch white pepper
3 sticks (24 tablespoons) cold unsalted butter,
   cut into 1-inch chunks
½ teaspoon fresh lemon juice

Preheat the oven to 275°F.

Heat the oil in a large cast-iron skillet over medium-high heat.

Cover both sides of the catfish with the Blackening Spice, pressing the spice into the fish with your hands.

When the skillet is hot, place the catfish fillets in the oil and sear on one side for 2 minutes, then turn and sear the other side for an additional 2 minutes. (You may cook the fillets in two batches if your skillet doesn't hold all 6 pieces of fish.)

Place the cooked fish in the preheated oven to keep warm while you are making the Beurre Blanc Sauce.

To make the Beurre Blanc Sauce: Bring the wine and vinegar to a boil in a small stainless steel saucepan.

Add the shallots, and salt and lower the heat to a simmer. Cook the liquid, stirring often, until it has reduced to about 2 tablespoons.

Remove the pan from the heat and whisk in 2 cubes of butter until the butter has melted. Return the pan to low heat and whisk in the remaining cubes of butter one at a time, allowing each cube to melt into the sauce before adding additional cubes.

Remove the sauce from the heat, add the white pepper, and whisk in the lemon juice.

Adjust to taste with salt and additional lemon juice, then strain through a fine sieve into a warm bowl.

Remove the Blackened Catfish from the oven and serve with the Beurre Blanc Sauce.

FRIED OYSTERS *with Red Pepper Sauce*

Serves 6

**1 pint (about 30) large Southern oysters,
    shucked and drained**
2 cups buttermilk
2½ cups yellow cornmeal
2½ cups all-purpose flour
**1 tablespoon Southern Seasoning Salt (recipe,
    page 188)**
1 teaspoon kosher salt
Vegetable oil, for frying

Red Pepper Sauce (recipe, page 18)

Preheat a deep cast-iron skillet on medium-
high heat, with 2 inches of vegetable oil, until
a probe thermometer reads 350° to 375°F.

Place all the oysters and the buttermilk in a
large bowl and set aside.

In a separate mixing bowl, whisk together
the cornmeal, flour, Southern Seasoning Salt,
and kosher salt until well blended.

Remove each oyster from the buttermilk,
one at a time, and add to the dry ingredients,
tossing to combine. Transfer each breaded oyster to a parchment-paper-lined baking sheet,
until all of the oysters are breaded.

Add the oysters to the hot oil, 5 or 6 at a
time, and cook until they are golden brown, no
more than 2 minutes. Use a skimmer or slotted
spoon to stir halfway through the cooking time.

Remove the oysters from the oil and drain
on a paper-towel-lined platter. Repeat the process until all of the oysters are fried.

Serve with Red Pepper Sauce on the side.

Roasted Oysters in Champagne

Serves 12

24 fresh oysters, in the shell
Rock salt
3 tablespoons salted butter
3 tablespoons all-purpose flour
1 cup Fish Stock (recipe, page 186)
½ cup brut Champagne
¼ cup heavy cream
2 tablespoons fresh flatleaf parsley, finely
chopped
1 tablespoon fresh thyme leaves
1 teaspoon chopped fresh dill
Freshly ground pepper, to taste

Shuck the oysters, reserving ½ cup of the juice from the oysters, and the 24 oyster shells.

Spread an even layer of rock salt on the bottom of a large oven-proof platter. Rinse and dry the 24 oyster shells and place atop the rock salt.

Melt the butter in a small heavy-bottom saucepan over medium-low heat.

Whisk in the flour and cook for about 2 minutes, whisking constantly. Do not let the roux brown.

Whisk the fish stock and the reserved juice from the oysters into the roux. Lower the heat and simmer gently for about 20 minutes, whisking often to prevent the sauce from sticking to the pan.

Whisk in ¼ cup Champagne and all the cream. Simmer the sauce for 20 minutes, whisking often, until the mixture is reduced to 1 cup.

Preheat the oven to 425°F.

In a separate saucepan, combine the remaining Champagne, parsley, thyme, and dill; and cook over medium heat for 10 minutes, until the liquid has reduced to 2 tablespoons.

Stir the herb mixture into the Champagne sauce and season to taste with black pepper. Reduce the heat to low.

Place one oyster in each shell and spoon a heaping teaspoon of the sauce over each oyster. Roast for 3 to 5 minutes and serve immediately.

SHRIMP & GRITS *with Tomato Okra Gravy*

Serves 4

2 pounds (about 30) large wild caught shrimp, peeled and deveined
1 cup yellow stone-ground grits
¾ cup shredded sharp cheddar cheese
¼ cup grated Parmesan cheese
2 tablespoons unsalted butter
2 tablespoons olive oil
4 slices thick cut bacon, cut into ¼-inch lardons, divided
1 small onion, chopped (about ½ cup)
1 clove garlic, minced
1 tablespoon all-purpose flour
½ cup vegetable or Chicken Stock (recipe, page 185)
2 medium garden fresh tomatoes, cored and diced (about 2 cups)
½ pound tender young okra, cut into ½-inch pieces (about 1½ cups)
Salt and freshly ground pepper, to taste
1 pinch cayenne pepper
1 tablespoon fresh lemon juice
4 scallions, thinly sliced

Season the shrimp with salt and pepper and set aside.

In a large heavy-bottom saucepan over high heat, bring 1 quart water to a boil. Reduce the heat to a simmer and whisk in the grits. Cover and cook for 30 minutes, whisking frequently, until the grits are tender and creamy. Add additional water if the grits are too thick.

Whisk in the cheddar, Parmesan cheese, and 1 tablespoon butter, and add salt to taste. Cover and set aside over low heat.

Heat the olive oil in a large cast-iron skillet over low heat, and cook the bacon for 10 minutes, stirring occasionally, until crisp. Use a slotted spoon to transfer the bacon to a towel-lined plate to drain.

Heat the remaining bacon fat in the skillet over medium-high heat. Add the shrimp and cook 2 minutes, turning once, until they are bright pink. Transfer the cooked shrimp to a plate and set aside

Lower the heat to medium-low, add the onions, and cook for 5 minutes, until they are soft but not yeet browned. Stir in the garlic and cook for 1 minute. Whisk in the flour continuously for 5 minutes until it is well incorporated, scraping the the bottom of the skillet as you go.

Increase the heat to high, add the chicken or vegetable stock and whisk until the gravy is smooth. Reduce the heat to low and simmer for 10 minutes, whisking occasionally, until the gravy thickens.

Add the tomatoes and okra to the gravy and bring it back to a simmer, stirring frequently. Cook for 7 to 10 minutes, until the okra and tomatoes soften, making a thick gravy.

Add the salt, black pepper, and cayenne pepper, and continue to simmer for 15 minutes, until the okra has cooked through. Add more stock if the gravy gets too thick.

Add the shrimp, lemon juice, and the remaining butter. Cook, stirring frequently, for 2 minutes, or until the shrimp heats through.

Divide the cooked grits between 4 bowls and top with the shrimp and tomato okra gravy. Garnish each bowl with the remaining lardons and scallions and serve warm.

Shrimp Bouchees

These small filled pastries are the ideal size for appetizers or passed hors d' ouerves.

Serves 6

**1 pound (about 40) small shrimp, peeled
and deveined**
**1 tablespoon Southern Seasoning Salt (recipe
page 188)**
1 sheet frozen puff pastry
¼ cup all-purpose flour
1 egg, lightly beaten with 1 tablespoon milk
1 tablespoon olive oil
½ cup chopped green onions
1 teaspoon Worcestershire sauce
1 teaspoon hot pepper sauce
1½ cup Shrimp Stock (recipe, page 187)
1 cup heavy cream
2 tablespoons cold unsalted butter
Salt and freshly ground pepper, to taste

Preheat the oven to 400°F.

Season the shrimp with Southern Seasoning Salt and set aside.

Roll the puff pastry out on a floured surface, to a ¼-inch thickness. Use a 3½-inch pastry cutter to cut out 12 circles.

Cut a smaller circle out of the center of 6 of the circles, leaving a ½inchwide rim of puff pastry.

Place the 6 full circles onto a parchment-lined baking sheet and brush with the beaten egg wash. Place the 6 circles, with the centers removed, on top of each of the full circles, matching up the edges.

Bake in the preheated oven for 10 to 15 minutes, or until the puff pastry has risen to about 3 times its original height and is golden brown. Remove from the oven and place on a platter or on individual plates.

Heat the oil in a large sauté pan over high heat, and sauté the shrimp for 2 to 3 minutes, until bright pink. Use a slotted spoon to remove from the pan and reserve.

Add the green onions, Worcestershire sauce, and hot pepper sauce to the pan, and cook for 1 minute.

Add the shrimp stock and bring to a boil, then reduce the heat to medium and simmer for 15 minutes, until the stock has reduced by half.

Add the cream and simmer for 10 minutes, until the sauce thickens enough to cover the back of a spoon. Add the reserved shrimp, whisk in the butter, and season with salt and pepper.

Divide the shrimp and sauce between each pastry bouchee and serve.

Herb & Dijon Crusted Rack of Lamb

★ ★ ★

MEAT & WILD GAME

· ·

Viandes & Jeu Sauvage

⚜ ⚜ ⚜

Lamb Shanks with Garlic & Butter Beans, page 93, and
Herb & Dijon Crusted Rack of Lamb, page 97

mint

lamb shanks

white wine

butter beans

thyme

tomato paste

Dijon mustard

breadcrumbs

garlic

flatleaf parsley

shallots

LAMB SHANKS *with Garlic & Butter Beans*

The slow-cooked butter beans make a rich, creamy sauce. This dish is an all-time family favorite at our house.

Serves 8

2 pounds dried butter beans, rinsed and soaked overnight in enough cold water to cover
8 lamb shanks
½ cup olive oil
1 cup Vegetable Stock, + 4 cups for the sauce (recipe, page 185)
5 large shallots, diced (about ⅓ cup)
8 large cloves garlic, minced
¼ cup brandy
3 large ripe tomatoes, diced (about 2 cups)
½ cup tomato paste
2 bay leaves
8 sprigs fresh thyme
4 cups white wine
Salt and freshly ground pepper, to taste

Preheat the oven to 325°F.

Heat 6 tablespoons olive oil in a large, deep sauté pan, or Dutch oven, over medium-high heat, and brown the lamb shanks on all sides Remove the shanks from the pan and set aside.

Drain the fat, and deglaze the pan using 1 cup vegetable stock. Pour the liquid into a small bowl and set aside.

Return the sauté pan to the stove, and heat the remaining 2 tablespoons oil over medium heat. Add the shallots and sauté for 2 to 3 minutes until translucent. Add the garlic and sauté for 1 additional minute. Add the brandy, tomatoes, tomato paste, bay leaves, and thyme and cook over low heat for 10 minutes.

Add the drained beans and arrange the lamb in the pan; with the meatier side down. Pour in the deglazing liquid, the wine, and the remaining vegetable stock.

Bring to a boil, then reduce the heat to medium-low and simmer for 15 minutes.

Cover the sauté pan with a tight-fitting lid and bake in the preheated oven for 1½ to 2 hours, or until the lamb shanks are fork tender and the beans are done. Check halfway through the cooking time and add more stock as needed.

Remove from the oven, discard the bay leaves and thyme, then increase the oven temperature to broil. Return the lamb to the oven and broil each side for 5 minutes to bown. Adjust the seasoning with salt and pepper.

Serve in a preheated bowl with the butter beans and sauce.

How to Make Herb & Dijon Crusted Rack of Lamb

1. Chop the fresh herbs.

2. Add the minced garlic.

5. Roll in the herbed breadcrumbs.

6. Press all the breadcrumbs onto the lamb rack.

3. Add the breadcrumbs.

4. Brush the seared lamb with mustard.

7. Place the pan in a hot oven.

8. Slice the lamb chops apart.

Herb & Dijon Crusted Rack of Lamb

Serves 8

4 tablespoons olive oil
1 cup Panko-style breadcrumbs
3 tablespoons finely chopped fresh mint
2 tablespoons finely chopped flatleaf parsley
3 cloves garlic, minced
2 French-cut racks of lamb (about 1½ pounds), trimmed
1 tablespoon salt
1 tablespoon freshly ground pepper
4 tablespoons Dijon mustard

Preheat the oven to 450°F.

Coat a roasting pan with 2 tablespoons olive oil and set aside.

In a small bowl, combine the breadcrumbs, mint, parsley, and garlic.

Season the lamb racks liberally with salt and pepper.

Heat the remaining olive oil in a large skillet over medium-high heat. Add 1 lamb rack to the pan at a time and sear for 6 minutes, turning after 3 minutes, so that each side browns.

Remove the lamb rack from the pan and repeat with the second rack of lamb.

Brush the Dijon mustard on all sides of the lamb racks, and use your hands to press the breadcrumb mixture over the lamb.

Place both breaded lamb racks in a roasting pan and bake for 18 minutes, or until a meat thermometer reads 135°F.

Remove from the oven and let the meat stand 10 minutes before slicing the racks into lamb chops.

PORK CHOPS, APPLES & FIGS

Serves 8

½ teaspoon crushed aniseed
1 teaspoon crushed fennel seeds
8 (6-ounce) boneless porkloin chops
Salt and freshly ground pepper, to taste
2 tablespoons olive oil
4 tablespoons unsalted butter
4 large shallots, thinly sliced
2 large cloves garlic, minced
2 tart apples, Granny Smith or Fuji, unpeeled
   and cut into ¼-inch-thick slices
¾ to 1 cup fresh orange juice
3 tablespoons fig preserves
2 tablespoons red wine vinegar

Sprinkle the aniseed and fennel seed on both sides of the pork chops and season overall with salt and pepper.

In a large cast-iron skillet, heat the olive oil on medium-high heat until very hot. Add the pork chops and sear for 3 minutes on each side, turning only once, until well browned.

Reduce the heat to medium and cook the pork another 4 minutes, until firm and barely pink inside. Transfer the meat to a plate and set aside.

Add 2 tablespoons of the butter to the same skillet over medium heat and swirl the pan until the butter has melted. Add the shallots, and cook for 4 minutes, until soft. Stir in the garlic and cook 1 minute.

Add the apple slices and cook for 2 minutes, stirring occasionally, until lightly browned.

Pour in ½ cup orange juice and cook for 1 minute, until the apple slices are just tender.

Add the fig preserves and the remaining orange juice, lower the heat to medium-low, and simmer for 5 minutes, stirring often to prevent the sauce from sticking and to blend the flavors.

Add the vinegar and season the sauce with salt and pepper.

Swirl the remaining butter into the sauce and return the pork and any juices left on the plate into the pan.

Increase the heat to medium and reheat the pork chops for 5 minutes.

Serve immediately.

PORK EN CROUTE *with Apple Duxelle*

A sweet and savory apple mixture replaces the traditional mushroom duxelle in this pork version of an en croute.

Serves 8

1 tablespoon unsalted butter, room temperature
1 pork loin (about 3 pounds)
1 tablespoon salt
1 tablespoon freshly ground pepper
1 tablespoon dried thyme
2 tablespoons vegetable oil
1 sheet prepared puff pastry, defrosted
1 large egg + 1 tablespoon of water, beaten
¼ cup all-purpose flour
⅓ cup Dijon mustard
3 cups Apple Duxelle (recipe follows)
1 tablespoon flaked sea salt

APPLE DUXELLE
1 cup Calvados
½ cup dried figs, diced
6 tablespoons unsalted butter
1 small onion, minced (about ½ cup)
4 large shallots, minced (about ¼ cup)
3 large cloves garlic, minced (about 1 tablespoon)
3 pounds assorted apples, such as Granny Smith, Fuji, Braeburn, peeled, cored and finely chopped
1 teaspoon salt
½ teaspoon freshly ground white pepper
2 tablespoons cider vinegar

Line a large baking sheet with parchment paper and set aside.

To make the Apple Duxelle: Combine the Calvados and dried figs in a small bowl and set aside.

Melt the 6 tablespoons butter in a large sauté pan over medium heat. When the butter has melted, add the onions, shallots, and garlic, and cook for 2 minutes, stirring occasionally.

Add the apples, salt, white pepper, and the Calvados fig mixture, and cook for 15 minutes, until the apples begin to caramelize, and any liquid has evaporated.

Add the cider vinegar and cook for 5 minutes, stirring continuously, to deglaze the pan.

Remove from the heat and set aside.

Season the pork loin on all sides with the salt, pepper, and thyme.

Heat 2 tablespoons oil in a large skillet over medium-high heat. Add the pork loin and sear all sides of the pork loin, turning frequently. Reduce the heat to medium and cook for 16 to 18 minutes, until a meat thermometer placed in the thickest part of the meat reaches an internal temperature of 110°F. Remove from the heat and cool for about 20 minutes.

Preheat the oven to 400°F.

Lightly flour a large surface and roll out the puff pastry to a 12x18-inch rectangle. Transfer the pastry to the parchment-paperlined baking sheet.

Place the pork loin lengthwise on the puff pastry, 1 inch from the edge of the pastry. Brush the pastry with a ½-inch border of egg wash along the edges.

Brush the pork loin, on all sides, with the mustard. Use your hands to firmly press the

See page 102 for How to Make Pork en Croute

cooled apple duxelle mixture over all the pork.

Gently pull the remaining pastry towards the pork loin to completely enclose the pork with the pastry. Gently press all edges together to completely seal the pork in the puff pastry.

With a small knife cut away any excess pastry to make an even border and crimp the pastry edges using a fork dipped in flour.

Brush the pastry evenly with the egg wash.

Make a decorative crosshatch pattern across the top of the pastry, using a small knife, and sprinkle with the flaked sea salt.

Bake in the preheated oven for 10 minutes, then turn the pan and bake an additional 10 to 15 minutes, until the pastry is golden brown. A meat thermometer placed in the thickest part of the meat should read an internal temperature of 150°F.

Remove from the oven and let the meat rest for 10 minutes before slicing.

How to Make Pork en Croute

1. Pat out the cold puff pastry.

2. Make and cool the Apple Duxelle.

3. Place the pork loin on one side.

7. Brush the edges with the egg wash.

8. Fold the pastry and parchment over the pork.

9. Unfold the parchment paper.

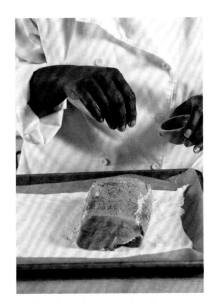

4. Season liberally.

5. Coat with mustard.

6. Top with the Apple Duxelle.

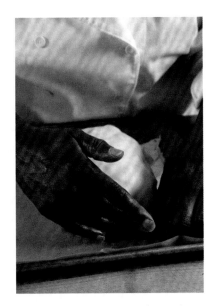

10. Press the pastry onto the pork loin.

11. Seal the edges.

12. Cut slits in the dough.

PULLED PORK *with Peppered Vinegar*

Serves 8

1 (5 pound) pork butt (also called pork shoulder)

RUB
¼ cup brown sugar
1 tablespoon chili powder
1 tablespoon smoked paprika
2 tablespoons garlic powder
2 tablespoons kosher salt
1 tablespoon freshly ground pepper
1 teaspoon cayenne pepper
4 onions, peeled and cut into halves
8 cloves garlic, smashed
2 cups Vegetable Stock (recipe, page 185)

Peppered Vinegar (recipe, page 191)

Stir together the brown sugar, chili powder, paprika, garlic powder, salt, black pepper, and cayenne in a small bowl. Set aside.

With a small paring knife, pierce the pork butt all over. Rub the spice mixture over the pork butt and wrap it tightly with plastic wrap. Refrigerate for at least 4 hours, but preferably overnight.

When you are ready to cook, preheat the oven or grill to 300°F.

Place the onion halves and smashed garlic in the bottom of a large Dutch oven.

Put the spice-rubbed pork on top and add the vegetable stock; cover with a tight-fitting lid and braise in the preheated oven, or grill for 4 hours, until the pork is fork tender and falling apart. (If using a charcoal grill, you may have to add more charcoal halfway through the cooking time.)

Let the pork rest, covered, at room temperature for 15 minutes before pulling.

Remove the lid and shred the meat using two forks, discarding any bones.

Serve with Peppered Vinegar on the side.

Pork Rillettes

More rustic than a liver pate, rillettes are made from lean meats slowly cooked in fat. The meat is then shredded and packed into jars, or ramekins, along with some of its cooking liquid and fat.

Serves 8

1 pound pork butt (also called pork shoulder), cut into 2-inch cubes
2 pounds pork belly, cut into 2-inch cubes
4 cups Vegetable Stock (recipe, page 185)
1 bouquet garni (recipe, page 65))
1 teaspoon salt
¼ teaspoon freshly ground pepper
1 pound pork fat, cut into thin slices

Place the cubed pork butt, cubed pork belly, the vegetable stock, and the bouquet garni in a large Dutch oven over low heat. Cover with a tight-fitting lid and cook for 4 hours, stirring occasionally, until the meat is fork tender.

Remove from the heat, discard the bouquet garni, and stir in the salt and pepper. Set aside until the pork is cool enough to handle.

Transfer the pork butt to a large bowl, discard any bones, and use two forks to shred the meat. Adjust the seasoning with salt and pepper.

Divide the shredded pork and braising liquid among several small jars; top each pork-filled jar completely with slices of pork fat. Cover each jar with a tight-fitting lid, or plastic wrap, and chill in the refrigerator for at least 3 days before serving. The flavors are enhanced as the Rillettes sits.

Serve as an hors d'oeurve, spread on toasted bread.

POT ROAST with Root Vegetables

Serves 8

1 (4-pound) boneless beef chuck roast, halved
¼ cup vegetable oil
Kosher salt
2 tablespoons unsalted butter
2 medium onions, peeled and diced (about 2 cups)
1 large carrot, peeled and diced (about 1 cup)
2 celery stalks, diced (about ¾ cup)
2 large garlic cloves, minced
1 cup Beef Stock + 2 cups for sauce (recipe, pages 184)
½ cup dry red wine + ¼ cup for sauce
1 tablespoon tomato paste
1 bay leaf
4 sprigs fresh thyme + ¼ teaspoon thyme leaves
Freshly ground pepper
1 pound carrots, peeled and cut crosswise into 2-inch pieces
1 pound turnips, peeled and cut into 2-inch pieces
1½ pounds Russet potatoes, peeled and cut into 2-inch pieces
1 tablespoon soy sauce

Pat the meat dry with paper towels, season liberally with oil, salt, and pepper, and let stand at room temperature for 1 hour.

Preheat the oven to 325°F.

Heat the oil in a heavy-bottom Dutch oven over high heat until very hot. Sear both pieces of meat for 5 minutes on each side, remove to a platter and set aside.

Reduce heat to medium-high and melt the butter in the Dutch oven. When it stops foaming stopped, add the diced onions and cook for 8 to 10 minutes, stirring occasionally, until they have softened and begin to brown.

Add the diced carrots and diced celery and continue to cook for 5 minutes. Add the garlic and cook about 30 seconds, until fragrant; be careful not to over-brown.

Stir in 1 cup stock, ½ cup wine, the tomato paste, bay leaf, and thyme. Increase the heat to medium-high and bring to a simmer.

Place the roasts in the Dutch oven with the vegetables, and cover with a tight-fitting lid. Cook for 3 hours; turning the roast after 1½ hours.

Add the carrots, turnips, and potatoes. Continue cooking for 30 minutes to 1 hour, until the beef is fork tender and the vegetables are cooked through.

Turn off the heat and use a slotted spoon to transfer the large pieces of carrot, turnip, and potato to a serving platter. Tightly cover with aluminum foil and set aside.

Transfer both pieces of the roast to a cutting board and tent loosely with aluminum foil.

Discard the bay leaf and thyme and puree the remaining vegetables in the Dutch oven with an immersion blender (or in a food processor, in batches; then return the sauce to the Dutch oven). Skim any fat from the surface. Add the remaining beef stock and bring to a simmer over medium heat.

Sice the roasts against the grain in ½-inch-thick slices. Transfer to a serving platter with the cooked vegetables.

Stir the chopped thyme, remaining wine, and soy sauce into the warm sauce and season to taste with salt and pepper. Pour half the sauce over the sliced pot roast and serve the remaining sauce on the side.

Beef in Red Wine Sauce

Serves 8

2 pounds trimmed beef chuck roast, cut into
  2-inch cubes
Salt and freshly ground pepper
1 tablespoon unsalted butter
2 tablespoons olive oil
1 large onion, finely chopped (about 1 cup)
3 cloves garlic, minced
1 tablespoon all-purpose flour
3 cups dry red wine
2 bay leaves
1 sprig thyme
6 ounces thick cut bacon, cut into
  1-inch lardons
1 cup pearl onions, peeled
2 cups cremini mushrooms
16 baby carrots, peeled
1 teaspoon sugar

GARNISH
¼ cup fresh flatleaf parsley, chopped

Preheat the oven to 350°F.

Season the cubes of chuck roast with salt and pepper and set aside.

Heat a large heavy-bottom stock pot over medium-high heat; add the butter and 1 tablespoon olive oil.

Add the beef and cook for 5 mnutes, turning occasionally, until browned on all sides.

Add the onion and garlic and cook over medium heat for 5 minutes, stirring occasionally, until the onion is softened.

Add the flour and stir to coat the meat chunks with it.

Add the wine, bay leaves, and thyme, and bring to a boil, stirring to dislodge the browned bits on the bottom of the pot. Season with salt and pepper.

Cover the stock pot with a tight-fitting lid and bake for 1 to 1½ hours, until the meat is fork tender.

In a large skillet over medium heat, heat the remaining olive oil. Add the lardons, pearl onions, mushrooms, and carrots, and cook for 10 minutes, until the lardons are crisp.

Add ¼ cup water and 1 teaspoon each of sugar, salt, and pepper.

Increase the heat to medium-high and bring to a boil, cover with a tight-fitting lid, then reduce the heat to low and simmer for 10 minutes, until the water has reduced by two-thirds and the vegetables are fork tender.

Uncover and cook an additional 5 minutes, until the vegetables have caramelized.

Remove the beef stew from the oven, stir in the vegetables, and garnish with the chopped parsley.

Serve with Buttermilk Whipped Potatoes (recipe, page 32).

CHARGRILLED STEAKS *with Scallion Butter*

When you're grilling a thick piece of meat, it's best to cook at a high temperature, to sear the outside nicely, then move to the cooler side of the grill.

Serves 8

8 (10-ounce) steaks (ribeye, NY strip, or fillet)
2 tablespoons olive oil
Sea salt and freshly cracked pepper, to taste

GARNISH
8 slices of cold Scallion Butter (recipe follows)

SCALLION BUTTER
8 ounces unsalted butter, room temperature
1 tablespoon scallions, both white and green parts, minced
3 cloves garlic, minced
1 tablespoon fresh flatleaf parsley, chopped
¼ teaspoon smoked paprika
½ teaspoon Worcestershire sauce
¼ teaspoon freshly cracked pepper
¼ teaspoon large grain sea salt

To make the Scallion Butter: Place all the ingredients into a bowl and thoroughly mix.

Using a rubber spatula to scrape the butter mixture onto a square of parchment paper, large enough to roll into a log. Twist the ends of the parchment to form a tight tube. Refrigerate until firm.

When ready to use, unwrap the parchment paper and slice into rounds.

To grill the steaks: Prepare a charcoal grill with high heat (about 450°F) on one side of the grill, and medium-low heat (about 300°F) on

the other. Use fewer briquettes on the cooler side of the grill to maintain the low heat. If using a gas grill, heat one side of the grill to the high heat and the other to the lower heat.

Remove the steaks from the refrigerator 30 minutes before you are ready to grill. Trim off any excess fat or gristle from the steaks and lightly brush both sides with olive oil; season liberally with salt and pepper.

Place the steaks on the hot side of the pre-heated grill, and cook for 45 seconds to 1 minute. Using a pair of tongs; turn the steaks over and sear the other side for the same amount of time. Searing the steaks on both sides seals in the juices.

Move the steaks to the cooler side of the grill, and continue to cook for 6 to 7 minutes for medium rare, or 8 to 9 minutes for medium. Turn the steaks halfway through the cooking time.

Transfer the steaks from the grill to a large platter to rest for 5 minutes before serving, so the juices can redistribute throughout the meat.

Garnish each steak with a round of Scallion Butter and serve.

Unused Scallion Butter can be frozen for up to 1 year, or refrigerated for 1 week.

Seared Ribeye Steaks with *Béarnaise Sauce*

Serves 8

BÉARNAISE SAUCE
¼ **cup white wine vinegar, or Shallot & Black Peppercorn Champagne Vinegar (recipe, page 21)**
¼ **cup dry white wine**
3 large shallots, minced (about 2 tablespoons)
3 tablespoons chopped fresh tarragon leaves, divided
Kosher salt
Freshly ground pepper
4 large egg yolks
8 ounce unsalted butter
Salt to taste
1 teaspoon lemon juice

8 (1-inch thick) ribeye steaks
Olive oil
Salt and freshly ground pepper, to taste

To make the Béarnaise Sauce: Combine the vinegar, white wine, shallots, black pepper, and 1 tablespoon tarragon leaves in a small stainless saucepan over medium heat. Bring to the first boil, then reduce the heat and simmer for 5 minutes, until there are only a few tablespoons of liquid left. Set aside to cool.

Fill a separate small saucepan with 2 inches of water, and bring to a boil over medium-high heat.

Put the cooled shallot mixture into a medium stainless steel bowl, and whisk in 1 tablespoon water and the egg yolks.

Turn the heat under the saucepan of water down to low, and place the bowl of eggs on top of the pan, making sure that it does not touch the water directly. Continue to whisk the yolks over the saucepan of hot water for 5 to 7 minutes, until they thicken. The volume of the yolks will almost double.

Add the butter, 1 or 2 tablespoons at a time, whisking slowly to emulsify. While you are doing this, occasionally remove the bowl from the pan to cool down the sauce and not scramble the eggs.

Taste the Béarnaise sauce and adjust the seasoning with salt and a splash of lemon juice. Stir in the remaining 1 teaspoon tarragon leaves. If the sauce is too thick, add hot water, 1 teaspoon at a time.

Let the sauce cool to room temperature before serving.

To make the Ribeye Steaks: Trim any excess fat or gristle from the steaks and lightly brush both sides with olive oil; season liberally with salt and pepper.

Heat ¼-inch layer of olive oil in a large sauté pan over high heat until it's almost smoking.

Sear the steaks for 1 minute on each side. Decrease the heat to low and cook the steaks for 6 to 7 minutes for medium rare, or 8 to 9 minutes for medium. Turn the steaks halfway through the cooking time.

Transfer to a large platter and loosely cover with aluminum foil. Let the steaks rest for 10 minutes to allow the juices to redistribute throughout the meat.

Serve the steaks with the Béarnaise Sauce on the side.

HOW TO MAKE RABBIT ROULADE

1. Add the cornbread to the pan.

2. Add the fresh herbs.

3. Mix well to combine.

6. Add the sausage and stuffing.

7. Fold the rabbit and bacon over the stuffing.

8. Place the seam side down in the pan.

4. Shingle the bacon.on a clean countertop.

5. Unfold the rabbit onto the bacon.

9. Roast until brown.

10. Slice evenly.

11. Serve hot.

RABBIT ROULADE *with Andouille Dressing*

Serves 4

2 rabbit loins (10 to 12 ounces each), (also
   called rabbit saddles), deboned
1 tablespoon unsalted butter
1 tablespoon olive oil
1 medium onion, finely diced (about 1 cup)
2 celery stalks, finely diced (about ½ cup)
1 small red bell pepper, finely diced (about
   ½ cup)
2 cloves garlic, minced
1 cup andouille sausage, diced
2 cups crumbled cornbread, recipe follows
2 teaspoons fresh thyme leaves
1 to 1½ cups Vegetable Stock (recipe,
   page 185)
Salt and freshly ground pepper, to taste
8 slices smoked bacon

BUTTERMILK CORNBREAD
¼ cup vegetable oil or bacon fat
1¼ cup cornmeal
¾ cup all-purpose flour
½ teaspoon baking powder
1 teaspoon salt
1 cup buttermilk
2 large eggs

To make the Buttermilk Cornbread: Preheat the
oven to 425°F.

Add the oil to an 8-inch cast-iron skillet and
place in preheated oven for 5 minutes.

In a large bowl whisk, together the cornmeal,
flour, baking powder, and salt, and set aside.

In a separate bowl, beat the buttermilk and
eggs until well blended, and stir in the hot oil
from the skillet. Add the flour mixture to the egg
mixture and stir until well combined.

Pour the batter into the prepared skillet. Bake
ifor 30 to 40 minutes, or until a toothpick inserted in the center comes out clean.

To make the Rabbit Roulade: Melt the butter
in a large sauté pan over medium heat. Add the
olive oil and stir to combine.
Add the onion, celery, bell pepper, garlic, and
andouille sausage and cook for 10 minutes, until the onion and celery are soft and translucent.

Mix in the crumbled cornbread and thyme;
season with salt and pepper and cook an additional 5 minutes, stirring often.

Add the stock and mix. Remove from the
stove and set aside to cool.

Preheat the oven to 375°F.

Shingle 4 slices of bacon on a clean, flat
surface. Spread the rabbit loin atop the bacon,
going in the same direction as the bacon; season liberally with salt and pepper.

Spoon half the sausage dressing down the
center of the rabbit loin. Firmly fold one side of
the rabbit over the sausage mixture, then fold
the opposite side over.

Fold one side of the shingled bacon over
the stuffed rabbit and repeat with the opposite
strips of bacon.

Place the stuffed rabbit loin, seam side down
into a large roasting pan. Repeat this process
with the second rabbit loin.

Bake in the preheated oven for 25 to 30
minutes, or until the internal temperature of the
stuffed loin reaches 160°F.

Remove from the oven and let the loins rest
for 10 minutes before slicing.

Tip:
If there are no hunters in your family, order a whole rabbit or rabbit loins from your grocer's butcher, or a famers' market. If you order a whole rabbit, make sure you get it with the head on.

garlic and bell pepper

andouille sausage

celery

wild mushrooms

rabbit

oyster mushroom

corn meal

parsley and thyme

cayenne peppers

Rabbit Roulade with Andouille Dressing, page 112, and **Braised Rabbit with Wild Mushrooms and Thyme**, page 115

Braised Rabbit with Wild Mushrooms & Thyme

Serves 4

1 whole (2½ to 3-pound) rabbit, cut
    into 8 pieces
Salt and freshly ground pepper, to taste
¼ cup all-purpose flour, for dusting
3 tablespoons olive oil
2 medium onions, finely diced
4 leeks, white and light green parts only,
    finely diced (about 2 cups)
6 cloves garlic, minced
2 tablespoons fresh thyme leaves
¼ cup dry porcini mushrooms, soaked in
    warm water to soften, drained, and finely
    diced
8 ounces cremini mushrooms, quartered
4 ounces shitake mushrooms, stemmed and
    quartered
1 cup chopped tomatoes
½ cup dry white wine
¼ teaspoon red pepper flakes
1 cup unsalted Chicken Stock (recipe, page 185)
2 ounces (½ stick) cold unsalted butter, cubed

Season the rabbit pieces with salt and pepper,
and dust lightly with flour.

Heat 3 tablespoons olive oil in a Dutch oven
over medium heat. Lightly brown the rabbit for
5 minutes on each side.

Remove the browned rabbit from the pan to
drain on paper towels, and set aside.

Preheat the oven to 350°F.

Add the onions to the hot Dutch oven and
cook for 5 minutes, until soft. Add the leeks,
garlic, thyme, and the mushrooms and cook for
10 minutes, stirring occasionally.

Add the chopped tomatoes and wine, and
let the mixture reduce for 5 minutes, stirring
occasionally. Season generously with salt and
pepper, and add red pepper flakes to taste.

Add the stock and bring to a simmer; adjust
seasoning with salt and pepper.

Add the browned rabbit pieces to the
mushroom mixture. Cover with a tight-fitting
lid and bake for 1 hour, or until the rabbit is
tender. Remove from the oven and let it rest for
10 minutes. Stir in the cold butter cubes just
before serving.

★ ★ ★

POULTRY

Volaille

⚜ ⚜ ⚜

STEWED HEN & FALL VEGETABLES

Hens are tougher than chicken so they need a long, slow cooking time to make them tender. It's worth the effort!

Serves 8

1 large stewing hen, cut into 10 pieces
  (2 legs, 2 thighs, 2 wings, 4 pieces of breast,
  saving the back and neck for stock)
Salt and freshly ground pepper
4 tablespoons unsalted butter
2 tablespoons olive oil
2 cups assorted mushrooms (such as shitake,
  morels, and cremini), quartered
6 cups Chicken Stock (recipe, page 185)
¼ cup tomato paste
1 sprig thyme
1 sprig rosemary
2 bay leaves
2 large cloves garlic, peeled and smashed
4 medium parsnips, peeled and cut into
  2-inch pieces (about 2 cups)
4 medium turnips, peeled and quartered
4 medium carrots, peeled and cut into 2-inch
  pieces (about 2 cups)
3 large celery stalks, cut into 2-inch pieces
  (about 1½ cups)
2 cups pearl onions, peeled
½ pound small new potatoes, halved or
  quartered

Liberally season the hen pieces with salt and pepper. Set aside.

Melt 2 tablespoons butter in a large Dutch oven over medium heat. When the butter stops foaming, stir in 1 tablespoon oil.

Add the mushrooms and cook for 10 minutes, until any liquid from the mushrooms has cooked off. Season with salt and pepper. Remove the mushrooms from the Dutch oven with a slotted spoon and set aside.

Add the remaining butter and oil to the hot Dutch oven. Add the hen and brown the pieces for 7 minutes on each side (add additional oil if cooking the hen in two batches).

Add the chicken stock, tomato paste, thyme, rosemary, bay leaves, and garlic and bring to a boil. Reduce the heat to low, cover with a tight-fitting lid and simmer for 2 hours.

Add the mushrooms, parsnips, turnips, carrots, celery, pearl onions, and potatoes and simmer for 20 minutes, until the vegetables are tender.

Remove the thyme and the bay leaves, and discard.

Adjust the seasoning with salt and pepper and serve.

garlic

thyme

mushrooms

rosemary

onion

tomato paste

oyster and shitake mushrooms

chicken leg quarters

carrots and celery

cognac (or brandy)

peppercorns

turnip

Stewed Hen & Fall Vegetables, page 118, and **Coq au Vin**, page 121

Coq au vin

This French classic is easier to make than you may think. It's a one-pot meal of stewed chicken, wine, bacon, and mushrooms—and a nice addition to your winter menu.

Serves 8

4 chicken leg quarters, separated
Salt and freshly ground pepper
2 tablespoons olive oil
4 slices thick-cut bacon, cut into ¼-inch
  lardons
2 cups cremini mushrooms, quartered
4 medium carrots, cut diagonally in 1-inch
  pieces (about 2 cups)
1 onion, halved and thinly sliced
2 large cloves garlic, chopped
¼ cup Cognac or brandy
½ bottle (375 ml) good dry red wine, such as
  a Burgundy
1 cup Chicken Stock (recipe, page 185)
10 sprigs thyme
2 tablespoons unsalted butter, room
  temperature, divided
1½ tablespoons all-purpose flour
2 cups pearl onions, peeled

Preheat the oven to 325°F.

Rinse and pat the chicken dry with paper towels, and liberally season with salt and pepper; set aside.

Heat the oil in a large Dutch oven over medium heat. Add the lardons and cook for 10 minutes, until lightly browned. Transfer the lardons to a large plate and set aside.

Add the chicken to the same pan over medium heat and brown for 5 minutes on each side. Remove the chicken from the pan and place on the same plate as the lardons, and set aside.

Melt 1 tablespoon butter in the same pan and cook the mushrooms for 10 minutes over medium-low heat until browned. Using a slotted spoon, transfer the mushrooms to a small bowl, and set aside.

Add the carrots and onions to the same pan, season them with salt and pepper, and cook over medium heat for 10 to 12 minutes, stirring occasionally, until the onions are lightly browned and the liquid has cookied out. Add the garlic and cook for an 1 additional minute.

Pour in the Cognac to deglaze the pan, stirring to loosen any brown bits on the bottom.

Return the lardons, chicken, and any juices that collected on the plate to the pot.

Add the wine, chicken stock, and thyme to the pot, and bring to a simmer.

Cover the Dutch oven with a tight-fitting lid and bake in the preheated oven for 30 to 45 minutes, until the chicken is cooked through. A meat thermometer placed in the thickest part of the thigh should reach an internal temperature of 165°F.

Remove the pot from the oven, keeping it covered, and place on top of the stove to cool for 10 minutes.

In a small bowl, mix the remaining butter and the flour together until well combined, and stir this into the stew. Add the pearl onions and browned mushrooms, and bring to a simmer over medium heat, and cook for an additional 10 minutes. Season to taste with salt and pepper.

Chicken Liver Pate *with Toast Points*

Serves 6

PATE
8 tablespoons unsalted butter, cubed
2 medium shallots, peeled and finely chopped
1 pound fresh chicken livers, membranes removed
1 tablespoon fresh thyme leaves, chopped
¼ cup brandy, or Cognac
3 tablespoons heavy cream + more as needed
Salt, to taste

TOAST POINTS
6 slices white bread, crusts removed
8 tablespoons salted butter, room temperature
Flaked sea salt

Melt half the butter cubes in a large, heavy sauté pan over medium-low heat.

Add the shallots and sweat for 5 minutes, until soft, being careful not to brown them. Add the chicken livers and thyme and cook for 5 minutes, until the livers are lightly browned on the outside but still very soft and pink on the inside.

Increase the heat to medium-high, add the brandy, and cook for a final 5 minutes.

Remove the pan from the stove, and let the chicken liver mixture cool slightly.

Transfer to a blender or food processor and add the cream and the remaining butter. Pulse until smooth; adding more cream as necessary.

Adjust the seasoning to taste with salt.

Spoon the pâté into small glass jars or containers. Cover with plastic wrap and refrigerate until firm, about two hours.

Chicken liver pate may be kept refrigerated for up to 1 week, or in the freezer for 2 months.

To make the Toast Points: Cut each slice of bread into 4 triangles.

Melt 4 tablespoons butter in a large sauté pan over medium heat.

Add 3 slices bread to the pan in a single layer, and cook 3 minutes on each side, until brown.

Remove the toast from the pan to drain on a paper-towel-lined sheet pan or platter.

Add the remaining butter and repeat the process with the remaining slices of bread.

Sprinkle with flake sea salt and serve with Chicken Liver Pate.

FRIED CHICKEN LIVERS

Serves 6

3½ cups buttermilk, divided
⅓ cup hot sauce
2 pounds chicken livers, membranes removed
3 cups all-purpose flour, divided
3 large eggs
2 teaspoons cayenne
2 teaspoons ground pepper
1½ teaspoons garlic powder
1 teaspoon paprika
2 teaspoons kosher salt
Oil, for frying
Flaked sea salt

In a large bowl, whisk 2 cups buttermilk with the hot sauce. Stir in the chicken livers; cover and refrigerate for at least 2 hours, or overnight.

Pour 1½ cups flour in a shallow bowl; set aside.

In a separate bowl, beat the eggs with the remaining 1½ cups buttermilk; set aside.

In a third bowl, mix the remaining 1½ cups flour, the cayenne, black pepper, garlic powder, paprika, and salt; set aside.

Remove the chicken livers from the buttermilk and dredge them first in the bowl of plain flour, one at a time.

Dip each liver into the egg mixture, turning to coat; then dredge them in the seasoned flour. Transfer to a cooling rack placed over a baking sheet.

In a large cast-iron skillet over medium-high heat, heat 2 inches oil to 350 to 375°F, measuring with a probe thermometer.

Add half the livers, one at a time, to the hot oil and fry for 3 to 5 minutes, turning, until golden. The chicken livers should be barely pink inside.

Drain on a paper-towel-lined platter and sprinkle with the flaked sea salt. Repeat with the remaining livers.

Serve piping hot.

SORGHUM GLAZED QUAIL

Sorghum or sorghum molasses, a Southern staple, is a thick, golden syrup that adds a depth of flavor not found in other sweeteners. It's also a powerhouse of nutrients.

Serves 6

12 whole quail, deboned
Salt and freshly ground pepper, to taste
2 tablespoons vegetable oil, for searing

MARINADE
½ cup cider vinegar
¾ cup olive oil
2 large cloves garlic, minced
¼ teaspoon red pepper flakes
2 sprigs thyme

GLAZE
⅓ cup sorghum
2 tablespoons Bourbon
1 tablespoon dark brown sugar

To make the Marinade: Combine the vinegar, oil, garlic, red pepper flakes, and thyme in a large bowl.

Set aside 2 tablespoons of the marinade (to use for the glaze) in a separate small bowl.

Add the quail to the large bowl of marinade, cover tightly with plastic wrap, and refrigerate for at least 1 hour, or overnight.

When you are ready to cook, preheat the oven to 425°F.

Remove the quail from the marinade and blot dry with a paper towel; season with salt and pepper and set aside.

To make the Glaze: Mix the 2 tablespoons reserved marinade, the sorghum, Bourbon, and sugar in a small saucepan. Cook over medium heat for 5 minutes, stirring constantly, until well combined. Remove from the heat and set aside.

Heat the 2 tablespoons vegetable oil in a large cast-iron skillet, over medium-high heat. Sear the quail, starting with the breast side down, for about 3 minutes, then turn and sear for 3 minutes on the other side, until nicely browned.

Remove the pan from the heat and brush each quail with half the glaze.

Place the skillet in the preheated oven and roast for 5 minutes, uncovered. Remove from the oven and let the quail rest for 5 minutes, then brush with the remaining glaze before serving.

Braised Quail with *Wild Mushrooms & Cognac*

Serves 4

8 whole quail, trussed
Salt and freshly ground pepper
4 tablespoons butter
2 tablespoons olive oil
4 large shallots, finely chopped (about ½ cup)
2 tablespoons all-purpose flour
½ cup Cognac
1 cup Chicken Stock (recipe, page 185)
¾ pound assorted wild mushrooms (such as
   chanterelles, morels, and cremini) trimmed
   and halved (about 2 cups)

GARNISH
2 tablespoons fresh flatleaf parsley leaves,
   coarsely chopped

Season the quail with salt and pepper, and set aside.

In a small Dutch oven over medium-high heat, melt 2 tablespoon butter with 1 tablespoon oil. Add the quail, and sear, starting breast side down, for 3 minutes on each side until nicely browned.

Remove the quail from the pan, and set aside.

Add the shallots to the pan and cook for 5 minutes, until brown.

Stir the flour into the shallots, and cook 1 additional minute.

Reduce the heat to medium-low.

Deglaze the pan with the Cognac (being careful if you're cooking over an open flame), stirring to loosen up the brown bits on the bottom of the pan.

Return the quail to the pan, add the stock, and cover with a tight-fitting lid. Braise the quail for 20 minutes, until just cooked through.

While the quail are braising, heat the remaining butter and oil in a large sauté pan over medium heat. When the butter has stopped foaming, add the mushrooms, season with salt and pepper; and cook for 15 minutes, until all the liquid is cooked off.

Remove the quail from the braising liquid and transfer to a serving platter. Cover loosely with aluminum foil to keep warm.

Bring the braising liquid to a boil over medium-high heat, and reduce, stirring, until the sauce thickens enough to coat the back of a spoon. Adjust to taste with salt and pepper.

Stir in the sautéed mushrooms.

Spoon the wild mushroom sauce over the platter of quail and garnish with chopped fresh parsley.

SOUTHERN CHICKEN POT PIE

Seasonal vegetables, tender chicken, and a flaky pie crust will make this dish a welcomed addition to any dinner table. Easily turn the leftover chicken from your French-style Roasted Rosemary & Lemon Chicken into this Southern style Chicken Pot Pie.

Serves 6

4 cups roasted chicken, diced
1 teaspoon fresh thyme leaves
Salt and freshly ground pepper, to taste
4 tablespoons olive oil
2 tablespoons unsalted butter
1 large onion, finely chopped
2 large cloves garlic, minced
3 medium parsnips, peeled and diced (about 2 cups)
3 medium carrots, peeled and diced (about 2 cups)
3 stalks celery, diced (about 1 cup)
1¾ cups Chicken Stock (recipe, page 185)
2 (9-inch) Pie Crusts (recipe, page 136)
2 tablespoons cornstarch
½ cup cream
2 cups fresh English peas, or frozen
¼ cup fresh flatleaf parsley, chopped
  + 1 tablespoon for garnish
Salt and freshly ground pepper, to taste
¼ cup melted butter

Preheat the oven to 425°F.

Season the diced roasted chicken with thyme, salt, and freshly ground pepper.

Add 2 tablespoons olive oil to a large sauté pan on medium-high heat. Add the diced chicken and cook for 5 minutes, or until lightly browned, stirring halfway through the cooking time. Transfer to a plate and set aside.

Heat the remaining olive oil and the butter in the same pan. Once hot, add the onion and cook for 5 minutes, until browned. Stir to loosen any browned bits from the bottom of the pan.

Add the garlic, parsnips, carrots, and celery, and cook for an additional 5 minutes, stirring constantly. Add the chicken stock, increase the heat to high and bring to a boil. Cover with a tight-fitting lid, and reduce the heat to a simmer. Cook for 10 minutes, or until the vegetables are tender-crisp.

While the vegetables cook, place one (9-inch) round of pie dough into a 3-inch deep pie pan; pressing the dough to the bottom and sides of the pan. Set aside.

In a small bowl, stir the cornstarch into the cream until it dissolves.

Stir the cream mixture into the vegetables in the pot and simmer for 5 minutes, stirring occasionally, until the sauce has thickened.

Add the peas, chopped parsley, diced chicken, salt, and black pepper to taste.

Bring the chicken and vegetable mixture back up to a simmer, then transfer to the dough-lined pie pan.

Place the second sheet of pie dough on top of the chicken and vegetable mixture, pressing the dough onto the edges of the pie pan.

Brush the top of the dough with the melted butter, and use a paring knife to make 5 evenly spaced, 2-inch slits through the pie dough.

Bake for 15 to 20 minutes, or until the pot pie crust is golden brown.

Garnish with parsley and serve piping hot.

Roasted Rosemary & Lemon Chicken

Fragrant rosemary, tart lemon, and fresh vegetables elevates this chicken recipe to the level sought after by French cooks. Using the French style of searing the skin at a high heat ensures it stays crisp, while finishing the dish at a lower temperature results in a tender juicy chicken.

Serves 6

1 (5 to 6 pound) roasting chicken
Kosher salt
Freshly ground pepper
10 stems fresh rosemary
10 stems fresh flatleaf parsley (save leaves for Southern Chicken Pot Pie)
1 lemon, halved
1 head garlic, cut in half crosswise
1 tablespoon olive oil
1 tablespoon melted butter
1 large yellow onion, peeled and quartered
4 carrots, peeled and cut into 2-inch chunks
2 celery stalks, cut in half

GARNISH
Juice of ½ lemon
2 tablespoons melted butter

Preheat the oven to 425°F.

Remove the chicken giblets, rinse the chicken inside and out, and remove any excess fat and leftover pin feathers. Pat the outside dry.

Liberally salt and pepper the inside of the chicken. Stuff the cavity with half the rosemary, all the parsley stems, both lemon halves, and all the garlic.

Truss the chicken, or tie the ends of the drumsticks together with butcher's twine, and tuck the wings under the body.

Brush the outside of the chicken with half the olive oil and half the melted butter. Liberally sprinkle with salt and pepper, rubbing the seasoning into the skin of the chicken.

Place the remaining rosemary, onions, carrots, and celery in a large roasting pan. Toss with salt and pepper and drizzle with the remaining olive oil and melted butter.

Place the chicken on top of the vegetables.

Roast the chicken for 30 minutes.

Remove from the oven and reduce the temperature to 350°F. Cover the breast with a triangle of folded aluminum foil and return to the oven.

Bake for 1 additional hour, until the juices run clear when you pierce the joint between the leg and thigh and a meat thermometer inserted into the thickest part of the thigh reads an internal temperature of 165°F.

Arrange the chicken and vegetables on a platter. Garnish the chicken by squeezing half the lemon over the entire roasted chicken, and brushing with melted butter.

Cover with a large sheet of aluminum foil and let rest for about 10 minutes before serving.

PERFECT PAN-FRIED CHICKEN BREASTS

This recipe makes some of the best fried chicken in the world. It isn't battered or deep fried but lightly dredged in well-seasoned flour and pan-fried until it is light, crisp, and juicy.

Serves 4

Vegetable oil for frying
Salt and pepper for seasoning
4 (6-ounce) chicken breasts
1 cup flour
1 tablespoon salt
2 teaspoons freshly ground pepper
1 tablespoon paprika

Add the vegetable oil to a depth of 1 to 1½ inches in a large cast-iron skillet with a lid, and heat to a temperature of 350° to 375°F.

Season the chicken breasts with salt and pepper and set aside.

Season the flour with additional salt, pepper, and paprika.

Dredge the chicken pieces through the seasoned flour.

Place the chicken breasts in the skillet of hot oil, cover, and fry for 20 minutes, until golden brown, turning once after the first 10 minutes.

Remove the lid, turn the chicken pieces over once more, and cook an additional 5 to 10 minutes to crisp up the skin.

Use a slotted spoon or spatula to transfer the chicken to a paper-towel-lined platter. Serve piping hot with Peppered Vinegar (recipe, page 191) or Red Pepper Sauce (recipe, page 18).

Fried Chicken Salad with Fresh Grapes
& Toasted Almonds

The addition of fresh grapes and toasted almonds adds a touch of elegance to a Southern favorite, making it a welcome addition to luncheons, picnics, and weeknight meals.

Serves 8

DRESSING
1 cup mayonnaise (recipe, page 183)
4 teaspoons apple cider vinegar
5 teaspoons honey
2 teaspoons poppy seeds
Salt and freshly ground pepper, to taste

SALAD
4 fried chicken breasts, diced
2 tablespoons olive oil
¾ cup slivered almonds, toasted
2 cups red or green seedless grapes, halved
3 stalks celery, thinly sliced
Salt and pepper, to taste

In a bowl, combine the mayonnaise, vinegar, honey, poppy seeds, salt, and pepper.

Refrigerate until you are ready to dress the salad. This can be prepared up to 2 days ahead.

Fry the chicken breasts (recipe, page 130), or use leftover fried chicken for this recipe.

Place the diced chicken in a large bowl and add almonds, grapes, celery, and dressing.

Stir to combine and adjust tthe seasoning with salt and pepper.

Serve chilled.

This salad is also delicious served on toasted baguette slices, or on a bed of fresh salad greens.

PAN-SEARED DUCK BREAST
with Whiskey Sauce

Serves 4

4 boneless duck breast halves, skin on
Salt and freshly ground pepper
2 tablespoons butter
2 shallots, finely chopped
1 cup freshly squeezed orange juice
2 tablespoons local honey
⅓ cup whiskey
2 tablespoons vegetable oil
2 tablespoons fresh orange zest, for garnish

Preheat the oven to 425°F.

Using a sharp paring knife, score the duck skin with a crisscross pattern, being careful not to cut into the meat. Season both sides liberally with salt and pepper and set aside.

Melt the butter in a small saucepan over medium heat. Add the chopped shallots and cook for 2 minutes, until soft. Add the orange juice, honey, and whiskey, and simmer for 5 minutes, stirring frequently, until the sauce has thickened to a syrupy consistency. Remove from the heat and set aside to cool.

Heat the vegetable oil in a large cast-iron skillet over medium-high heat. Add the duck breasts, skin-side-down, and cook for 5 minutes, or until the majority of the fat has been rendered from the duck skin.

Remove the skillet from the heat and pour off the excess fat. Turn the duck breasts skin-side-up in the skillet and place it in the oven.

Roast the duck for 8 to 10 minutes, until the skin is crisp, and a meat thermometer inserted into the thick part of the duck reads an internal temperature of 150°F.

Let the duck stand for 5 minutes before cutting into ¼-inch slices.

Place the sliced duck breasts on a platter, reheat the whiskey sauce, and spoon it over the duck.

Garnish with orange zest and serve.

Duck Confit

Confit is a preservation method. Cooking and keeping duck in its rendered fat results in meltingly tender, moist, and extremely flavorful meat which can be used in a variety of simple preparations. Rendering duck fat gives you 'liquid gold' and a batch of duck crackling. Sprinkle with sea salt for a delicious treat.

Serves 4

½ cup sea salt
2 tablespoons coarse pepper, freshly ground
½ cup dark brown sugar
4 dried bay leaves, broken into small pieces
4 duck (leg-and-thigh) quarters
10 sprigs thyme
4 large cloves garlic, chopped
4 cups rendered duck fat, recipe follows

Day 1. In a small bowl, combine the salt, pepper, sugar, and bay leaves, and use half the mixture to sprinkle the duck quarters generously. Place the duck quarters in a 9x13-inch casserole dish in one layer. Cover tightly with plastic wrap and refrigerate for 24 hours.

Day 2. Sprinkle 1 tablespoon of the reserved salt mixture in the bottom of a 9x13-inch casserole dish. Arrange half the garlic and the sprigs of thyme evenly in the bottom of the baking dish, and add the duck quarters, skin-side-up, atop the garlic and thyme. Sprinkle the leg quarters with the remaining salt mixture, and the remaining garlic and thyme. Cover with plastic wrap and refrigerate for another 24 hours.

Day 3. Remove the duck legs and quarters from the refrigerator and rinse the salt and herbs off. Position the duck skin-side-up on a cooling rack placed over a baking sheet.

Place in the refrigerator, uncovered, for a final 24 hours.

Day 4. Preheat the oven to 225°F.

Arrange the duck quarters in a single layer in a 9x13-inch baking dish.

Melt the rendered duck fat in a small saucepan and pour over the duck; the duck pieces should be totally covered by fat.

Place in the preheated oven and cook for 2 to 3 hours, until the duck is tender and can be easily pulled from the bone. Remove the duck confit from the oven. Cool and store the duck in the fat until you are ready to eat.

To serve, remove the duck from the fat, place on a baking sheet in a preheated 425°F oven, and cook for 10 minutes, or until the skin is crisp. The duck confit will keep refrigerated for up to 6 weeks. Note: The duck fat can be strained, cooled, and reused.

RENDERED DUCK FAT
Yields scant 4 cups
Skin and fat from 2 whole ducks

Cut the skin and fat into 2-inch pieces and put into a medium, heavy-bottom saucepan over medium heat.

Add ¾ cup water and bring to a low simmer. Cook for 1 hour, until the water evaporates and the skin is crisp and has rendered all the fat.

Strain the fat through a fine sieve.

Store the rendered duck fat in a sealed container in the refrigerator for up to 3 months.

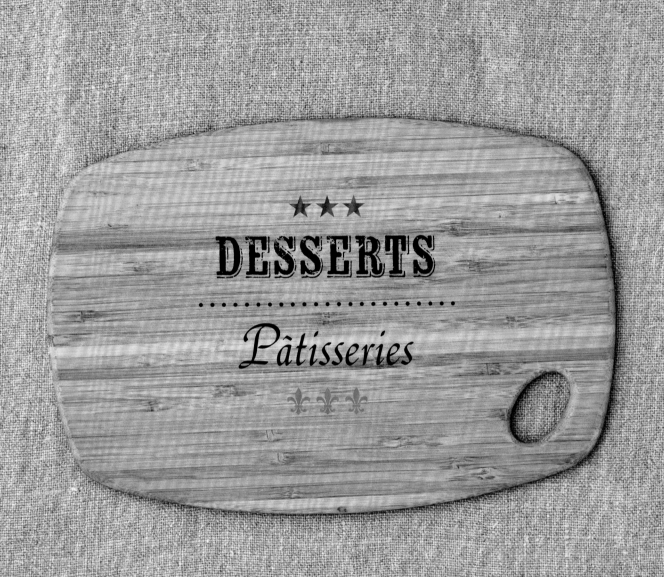

★ ★ ★

DESSERTS

· ·

Pâtisseries

⚜ ⚜ ⚜

CHERRY PIE *with Chantilly Crème*

Serves 8

LATTICE PIE CRUST (or double crust)
2½ cups all-purpose flour
1 tablespoon sugar
¾ teaspoon salt
1 cup unsalted butter, cold, cut into
   ¼-inch cubes

CHERRY FILLING
1 cup plus 1 tablespoon sugar
3 tablespoons cornstarch
¼ teaspoon salt
5 cups whole pitted dark sweet cherries
   (about 2 pounds, unpitted)
3 tablespoons fresh lemon juice
½ teaspoon vanilla extract
2 tablespoons unsalted butter, cold, cut
   into ¼-inch cubes
1 tablespoon milk

GARNISH
2 cups Chantilly Crème (recipe, page 142)

To make the Lattice Pie Crust: Whisk the flour, sugar, and salt together in a large bowl. Cut in the cold butter using a pastry cutter or two forks, until it resembles coarse cornmeal.

Add 5 tablespoons cold water and mix with a fork until a loose dough forms, adding additional teaspoons of cold water if the dough is dry.

Turn the dough out onto a lightly floured surface and knead for 5 minutes, until the dough comes together. Divide the dough in half and flatten into 2 disks. Wrap each disk separately in plastic wrap. Refrigerate for at least 30 minutes.

Remove the dough from the refrigerator and let it soften at room temperature for 10 minutes before rolling out.

On a lightly floured surface, roll out one dough disk into a 12-inch round. Transfer it to a 9-inch pie pan, trim the overhanging dough to ½-inch around, and set aside.

Roll out the second dough disk to a 12-inch round. Using a paring knife or fluted pastry wheel, cut twelve ½-inch wide strips from the dough, and arrange in a lattice design on a separate piece of parchment paper. Set aside.

Preheat the oven to 425°F.

To make the Cherry Filling: Whisk together 1 cup sugar, cornstarch, and salt in a medium bowl. Stir in the cherries, lemon juice, and vanilla. Pour the filling into the prepared pie crust, mounding slightly in the center, and dot with butter.

Drape the lattice dough design over a rolling pin to transfer it to the top of the pie. Trim the dough strips to overhang the pan to ½-inch around. Fold the overhanging bottom dough up over the hanging strips of the lattice and pinch the edges to seal.

Brush the lattice dough, but not the edges, with milk, and sprinkle with the remaining 1 tablespoon sugar.

Place the cherry pie on a baking sheet and bake in the preheated oven for 15 minutes.

Reduce the oven temperature to 375°F and bake an additional 1 hour, until the pie filling is bubbling and the crust is golden brown. Cover the crust edges with aluminum foil if they are browning too quickly.

Remove from the oven and transfer the pie to a cooling rack for 2 hours, to cool completely.

Serve with Chantilly Crème.

butter

Cherry Pie with Chantilly Crème, page 136, and Profiteroles with Brandied Cherry Sauce, page 138

salt

flour

sugar

eggs

cream

vanilla

cherries

Profiteroles with Brandied Cherry Sauce

Filled with whipped cream, pastry cream, or Chantilly Crème, these French pastries are versatile and easy to prepare.

Serves 8

½ cup whole milk
½ cup unsalted butter, cut into 8 pieces
1 teaspoon + 2 tablespoons sugar
1 teaspoon kosher salt
1 cup all-purpose flour
5 large eggs, room temperature, + 1 large egg
   for egg wash
2½ cups heavy cream
2 cups Brandied Cherry Sauce (recipe,
   page 139)

Preheat the oven to 450°F.

Line 2 baking pans with parchment paper and set aside

Fit 1 large pastry bag with a plain ½-inch pastry tip and set aside.

In a medium saucepan over medium heat, add the milk, butter, 1 teaspoon sugar, salt, and ½ cup water and bring to a boil, stirring occasionally.

Reduce the heat to medium-low and add the flour all at once. Stir vigorously with a wooden spoon for 2 minutes, or until a thick dough forms and pulls away from the sides of the saucepan. Continue vigorously mixing the dough 1 additional minute, until it begins to dry out.

Transfer the dough to a large bowl and beat in one egg at a time for 2 minutes each, mixing each egg until well combined and the dough looks dry, before adding the next egg. When all the eggs have been added, the dough should look smooth and shiny.

Spoon the dough into the prepared pastry bag and pipe 16 (2½-inch) rounds out onto the parchment-lined baking pans, leaving 2 inches between rounds. Set aside.

Whisk the remaining egg with 2 teaspoons water and brush the dough rounds with the egg wash.

Transfer the profiteroles to the preheated oven, then turn the oven off and leave the baking sheets in the hot oven for 10 adittional minutes.

After 10 minutes, turn the heat to 350°F and bake for 10 minutes.

Rotate the pans front to back and top to bottom and continue baking 10 more minutes, until the profiteroles are deep golden brown all over. Note: They will deflate if removed from the oven before fully baked.

Transfer the baking sheets to a wire rack for at least 15 minutes to cool completely.

Using a serrated knife, gently slice the top quarter off each puff and place on individual plates; reserve the tops on a plate.

With your finger, gently push down the soft film of cooked dough inside each puff.

Whisk the heavy cream in a large bowl with the remaining 2 tablespoons sugar until soft peaks form. Spoon the whipped cream into each profiterole, add a heaping tablespoon of brandied cherry sauce, and cover with profiterole tops.

Serve immediately.

Brandied Cherry Sauce

Yields about 3½ cups

¾ **pound fresh dark sweet cherries**
⅓ **cup sweetened cherry juice**
¼ **cup sugar**
1 tablespoon arrowroot
¼ **cup brandy**

Pit and halve the cherries.

In a medium saucepan, combine the cherries, cherry juice, and sugar over medium-high heat and bring to a simmer.

Simmer the cherries for 5 minutes, stirring occasionally, until they soften slightly.

In a small bowl, mix the arrowroot and brandy together and stir into the cherry mixture. Cook on low heat for an additional 5 minutes, then remove from the heat and let it cool completely. Serve with the Profiteroles. This sauce is also good with the Shortbread (recipe, page 148).

APPLE SPICE CAKE

The smell of baking Spice Cake always makes me think of Fall—so full of spices, brown sugar, and ripe fall apples.

Serves 12

½ cup raisins
2 cups all-purpose flour + 1 tablespoon to flour Bundt pan
1 teaspoon cinnamon
1 teaspoon nutmeg
1 teaspoon ginger
1 teaspoon allspice
½ teaspoon salt
1 cup unsalted butter, softened + 1 tablespoon to grease Bundt pan
1 cup sugar
1 cup dark brown sugar, firmly packed
4 large eggs, room temperature
1½ teaspoons vanilla extract
1 teaspoon baking soda
3 large Granny Smith apples, peeled, cored and coarsely chopped
½ cup warm water + 1 tablespoon
½ cup walnuts, coarsely chopped
3 cups Cream Cheese Frosting, recipe follows

CREAM CHEESE FROSTING
Yields about 4 cups

½ cup butter, softened
8 ounces cream cheese, room temperature
4 cups powdered sugar, sifted
2 teaspoons vanilla extract

Preheat the oven to 350°F.

Butter and lightly flour a 9-inch Bundt pan.

In a small bowl, cover the raisins with ½ cup warm water, let them soak for 10 minutes, then drain and set aside.

In a separate bowl, sift together the flour, cinnamon, nutmeg, ginger, allspice, and salt. Set aside.

In another bowl, cream together the butter and both sugars for 5 minutes until light and fluffy. Pour the eggs and vanilla into the butter and sugar, mixing until well combined.

Stir together the baking soda and 1 tablespoon warm water, and mix into the creamed butter and sugar.

Toss the apples, drained raisins, and walnuts together in the flour and spice mixture until well coated with flour. Combine the creamed butter and apple/raisin flour mixtures together, stirring until well combined. The cake batter will be very thick.

Pour the batter into the prepared pan and bake for 1 hour, or until a wooden toothpick inserted into the cake comes out clean.

Remove from the oven and place on a wire rack for 10 minutes. Shake the pan to loosen the cake, and turn out onto the wire rack to cool completely for 1 additional hour.

Place on a cake plate to ice with the cream cheese frosting.

To make the Cream Cheese Frosting: Beat the softened butter and cream cheese together until well blended. Beat in the powdered sugar, 1 cup at a time. Add the vanilla and beat until smooth and creamy.

Poached Spiced Apples *with Chantilly Crème*

Serves 4

1½ cups fruity red wine, such as Syrah or Zinfandel
¾ cup sugar
½ cup fresh orange juice
2 (3x1-inch) strips fresh orange peel, pith removed
1 (3x1-inch) strip fresh lemon peel, pith removed
1 cinnamon stick
2 whole star anise
4 medium Pink Lady or Braeburn apples, peeled and cored
1 cup Chantilly Crème (recipe, page 142)

Combine the wine, sugar, orange juice, orange and lemon peels, the cinnamon stick, star anise, and 2 cups water in a large heavy-bottom saucepan over medium heat.

Bring to a rolling boil, stirring until the sugar has dissolved.

Submerge the apples carefully in the boiling liquid and reduce the heat to low, simmering for 25 to 30 minutes, occasionally rotating the apples, until they are fork tender. Remove them from the poaching liquid and set aside.

Strain the poaching liquid into a smaller saucepan, discard the citrus peels and spices, and return the saucepan to medium heat.

Simmer for 10 to 15 minutes, stirring occasionally, until the poaching liquid is thick and syrupy, and has reduced to about ¾ cup. The syrup will thicken more as it cools.

Divide the Chantilly Crème among four plates, place a warm apple on top of the cream and drizzle with the spiced syrup.

Serve warm.

Chantilly Crème

This classic French crème is made with sweetened fresh cream and a hint of vanilla. Chantilly Crème adds an unexpected richness to pies, pastries, and hot drinks.

Yields 2 cups

1 cup heavy whipping cream
½ teaspoon vanilla extract
3 tablespoons powdered sugar

Pour the cream and vanilla into a small chilled copper or glass bowl and whisk for 5 minutes, until it begins to thicken.

Sprinkle the powdered sugar into the cream and vanilla and continue to whisk vigorously for 10 minutes, until soft peaks form.

Chill until ready to use.

LEMON MERINGUE PIE

For a super high meringue, make sure you whip your egg whites in a clean, dry metal or glass bowl. No plastic!

Serves 8

PIE FILLING
4 large egg yolks, room temperature, whites reserved for the topping
⅓ cup cornstarch
1⅓ cups sugar
¼ teaspoon salt
3 tablespoons butter
½ cup fresh lemon juice
1 tablespoon fresh lemon zest

1 (9-inch) pie crust (recipe, page 156)

MERINGUE TOPPING
4 reserved egg whites
⅛ teaspoon cream of tartar
2 tablespoons sugar

Prepare a 9-inch pie shell.

Preheat the oven to 375°F.

In medium mixing bowl, whisk the egg yolks and set aside.

In a medium heavy-bottom saucepan, whisk together the cornstarch, 1½ cups water, sugar, and salt.

Place the saucepan on medium heat, bring to a boil, and boil for 1 minute, stirring frequently. Remove from the heat and slowly add ¼ cup hot mixture to the bowl of egg yolks, whisking constantly. This will temper the yolks and prevent the eggs from scrambling.

Gradually whisk the remaining hot mixture into the egg yolks.

Return the egg mixture to the saucepan over low heat and cook, stirring constantly, for 1 additional minute. If the egg yolks scramble, strain through a fine sieve and discard any solids.

Remove from the heat and stir in the butter. When the butter melts, stir in the lemon juice, and zest, and mix well.

Pour the mixture into the prepared pie shell and set aside.

To make the Meringue Topping: Add the egg whites and cream of tartar to a large bowl, and use a whisk or an electric mixer with beater attachments to beat until soft peaks form. Gradually add the sugar and continue beating for 1 to 2 minutes, until stiff peaks form.

Using a rubber spatula, spread the meringue over the pie filling to the edge of the crust so that it completely covers the filling. Use the spatula to make peaks and curls in the meringue.

Bake for 10 to 12 minutes, until the meringue is golden.

Remove the pie from the oven and cool on a wire rack for at least 1 hour.

Place the cooled pie in the refrigerator and chill for at least 1 hour before serving.

Tarte au Citron

Too-cold dough can crack and split when rolled; let this sit at room temperature for five minutes before you roll it out.

Makes 1 (9-inch) tart

1 cup freshly squeezed lemon juice
2 large lemons, zested
¾ to 1 cup sugar
12 tablespoons unsalted butter, cut into
   ½-inch cubes
4 large eggs, room temperature
4 large egg yolks, room temperature
1 pre-baked (9-inch) tart shell, recipe follows

GARNISH
1 lemon, thinly sliced into rounds
2 tablespoons superfine sugar

TART DOUGH
2 tablespoons dark brown sugar
½ teaspoon kosher salt
1 cup all-purpose flour + ¼ cup for kneading
6 tablespoons cold unsalted butter, cut into
   ¼-inch pieces
1 large egg, beaten

To make the Tart Dough: Preheat the oven to 350°F.

Whisk together the sugar, salt, and 1 cup flour in a medium bowl. Cut in the butter, using a pastry cutter or 2 stainless steel knives, until the mixture resembles coarse cornmeal. Drizzle the beaten egg over the dough and mix gently with a fork until the dough comes together in a loose ball.

Turn the dough out onto a lightly floured surface and knead for 5 minutes, until smooth. Form the dough into a flat disk, wrap it tightly in plastic wrap, and chill for at least 2 hours, until firm.

When it has chilled, unwrap the dough and roll it into a 12-inch disk on a lightly floured surface to keep the dough from sticking.

Place the disk into a 9-inch tart mold with a removable bottom, and use your fingertips to pat it into the pan and up the sides. Trim and remove any excess dough.

Prick the dough all over with the tines of a fork and bake in the preheated oven for 15 minutes, until the dough is golden brown.

Remove from the oven and let the tart shell cool on a rack until ready to use.

To make the garnish: Preheat the oven to 350°F. Place the sliced lemon on a parchment-lined baking pan, sprinkle with the superfine sugar, and bake for 5 to 10 minutes, until the lemon has browned. Let it cool, and set aside.

To make the filling: In a heavy-bottom stainless steel saucepan, over medium-low heat, combine the lemon juice, zest, ¾ cup sugar, butter, eggs, and egg yolks. Taste and adjust the sweetness with the remaining ¼ cup sugar, if needed. Stir until the butter melts, then continue to cook for 10 minutes, whisking constantly, as the mixture thickens into a thick paste. The lemon mixture should hold its shape when held right-side-up on the whisk.

Pour the warm lemon curd into the prebaked tart shell, spread, and smooth the surface.

Bake in the preheated oven for 5 to 6 minutes, until the curd is just set. Remove from the oven and transfer to a cooling rack for at least 30 minutes.

Garnish with the baked lemon slices.

STRAWBERRY LEMON CAKE

Serves 12

1 cup unsalted butter, softened + 2 tablespoons
  for cake pans
3 cups cake flour + 2 tablespoons for cake
  pans
1 tablespoon baking powder
1/8 teaspoon table salt
2 cups sugar
4 large eggs, room temperature, separated
1 cup milk
1 tablespoon fresh lemon zest
1 tablespoon fresh lemon juice
2 cups Strawberry Lavender Preserves (recipe,
  page 19)
Strawberry Icing, recipe follows

GARNISH
5 strawberries, hulled and sliced

STRAWBERRY ICING
Yields about 4 cups

1 pound cream cheese, softened
2/3 cup sugar, divided
1½ cup fresh strawberries, coarsely chopped
2 cups heavy cream
3 tablespoons fresh lemon juice

Preheat the oven to 350°F.

Butter and lightly flour 4 (9-inch) cake pans and set aside.

In a medium bowl, sift together the flour, baking powder, and salt and set aside.

Fit an electric mixer with the paddle or beater attachment and beat 1 cup butter at medium speed until creamy. Gradually add the sugar to the creamed butter, beating until the batter is light and fluffy. Add the 4 egg yolks, 1 at a time, beating until well combined after each addition.

Add the flour mixture to the creamed butter and sugar mixture, alternating with the milk; beginning and ending with the flour mixture.

Beat at low speed, just until blended; stir in the zest and lemon juice, and set aside.

In a separate bowl, beat the 4 egg whites on high speed until stiff peaks form. Stir one-third of the egg whites into the cake batter, then gently fold in the remaining egg whites.

Spoon the cake batter into the 4 prepared cake pans and bake for 16 to 20 minutes, or until a wooden toothpick inserted in the center comes out clean.

Remove the pans from the oven and let them cool on a wire rack for 10 minutes.

Gently remove the cake from the pans, place on the wire racks, and cool for another 30 minutes, or until they have completely cooled.

To make the Strawberry Icing: Fit an electric mixer with the paddle or beater attachments and beat the cream cheese and 1/3 cup sugar in a medium bowl until smooth.

Add the strawberries and beat until well blended; set aside.

In a separate large bowl, beat the heavy cream and lemon juice until foamy. Slowly add the remaining 1/3 cup sugar, and beat until stiff peaks form.

Using a rubber spatula, fold half the whipped cream mixture into the strawberry cream cheese mixture. Scrape the sides and bottom of the bowl, and fold the remaining whipped cream mixture into the strawberry cream cheese mixture.

Cover with plastic wrap, refrigerate at least 1 hour, and reserve to ice the Strawberry Lemon Cake. Remove the icing from the regrigerator 30 minutes before frosting the cake.

When you are ready to frost the cake, place 1 cake layer on a serving platter, and spread 1 cup Strawberry Icing and top with about ½ cup Strawberry Lavender Preserves, leaving a

½-inch border around the edges.

Repeat with the second and third cake layers, spreading the preserves and icing between each layer.

Spread the remaining 2 cups Strawberry Icing on the top and sides of the cake.

Garnish the cake with sliced strawberries.

Frozen Strawberry Soufflé

This recipe is a fun, no-bake version that guarantees your soufflé will never fall.

Yields 6 (4-ounce) soufflés

1 tablespoon powdered gelatin
2 cups heavy whipping cream, cold
2 quarts fresh strawberries, hulled
1¾ cups sugar
¼ teaspoon salt
2 teaspoons vanilla extract

Fold 1 (15x21-inch) sheet of parchment paper into thirds, and cut into 6 (3 x 8-inch long) strips. Wrap each 3-ply strip around a ramekin so that it extends above the rim by about 2 inches, secure in place with Scotch tape, and place the ramekins on a rimmed baking sheet.

Pour 3 tablespoons lukewarm water into a small cup and sprinkle with the powdered gelatin, do not stir. Set aside for 20 minutes to allow the gelatin to dissolve.

In a separate medium bowl, beat the heavy cream into stiff peaks and set aside.

Fit a food processor with the blade attachment, and process the strawberries and sugar for 2 minutes, until the sugar is completely dissolved. Add the salt and vanilla, and pulse to incorporate. Pour the pureed strawberry mixture through a fine sieve into a large bowl. Using a rubber spatula, press out all the juice and discard the seeds.

Add the gelatin mixture to the bowl and whisk until well incorporated.

Fold in the heavy cream.

Divide the strawberry mixture evenly into the ramekins on the baking sheet, filling to the top of the parchment paper, and freeze for at least 3 hours.

Remove from the freezer 10 minutes before serving, remove the parchment paper, and serve cold.

SHORTBREAD *with Peach Preserves*

I know that the French have a reputation for making some of the best pastries in the world, but I have to say that they've met their match against our Southern desserts. The long growing season gives Southerners fresh fruits and vegetables to use in our desserts. Everything from peaches to apples and cherries becomes cakes, cobblers, and pies.

Serves 6

4 cups all-purpose flour
2 tablespoons sugar
2 tablespoons dark brown sugar
½ teaspoon salt
1 tablespoon + 2 teaspoons baking powder
5 tablespoons + 1 teaspoon cold unsalted
   butter, cut into ¼-inch cubes
1¼ cups heavy cream
¼ cup melted unsalted butter
2 cups Peach Preserves (recipe, page 149)

GARNISH
1 cup Chantilly Crème (recipe, page 142)

Preheat the oven to 450°F.

In a large mixing bowl, sift together the flour, sugar, brown sugar, salt, and baking powder until well combined.

Use a pastry cutter or 2 stainless steel forks to cut in the cold butter, a few cubes at a time, until the mixture resembles coarse cornmeal.

Pour in the cream all at once, and stir until the dough is soft.

Knead the dough on a lightly floured surface for about 1 minute, or until the dough comes together. Be careful not to over-knead.

Roll the dough out to ½-inch thick, and use a 3½-inch biscuit cutter to cut out 10 to 12 shortbreads. Place the shortbread rounds on a baking sheet and brush the tops with the melted butter.

Bake in the preheated oven for 10 to 15 minutes, or until golden brown.

Remove from the oven, and cut each shortbread in half. Place the bottom halves on a plate, cover with ⅓ cup Peach Preserves, and add a shortbread top to each.

Garnish with Chantilly Crème and serve.

PEACH PRESERVES

Yields about 2 pint jars

3 pounds ripe peaches
1 tablespoon lemon juice
2 cups sugar
1 teaspoon salt

To blanch the peaches: Bring 2 quarts water in a large stockpot to to a boil over medium-high heat. Add the peaches, and boil for 30 to 45 seconds, then use a slotted spoon to remove the peaches and immediately submerge them in a large bowl of ice water.

Remove the peaches and pat dry.

Use either a vegetable peeler or a paring knife to peel the skin from the peaches. Cut them in half and remove the pits. Slice each peach half into 5 or 6 slices and set aside; discard the peels and pits.

Place the peach slices, lemon juice, sugar, and salt in a large heavy-bottom stainless steel saucepan over medium heat and bring to a boil.

Continue to boil for 25 to 30 minutes, stirring occasionally, until a thermometer placed in the liquid shows a temperature of 220°F.

Remove the saucepan from the heat and ladle the hot preserves into 4 sterilized pint jars, leaving a ¼-inch space from the rim of the jar.

Wipe the rim, add a sanitized lid, and tighten until fingertip tight; do not overtighten.

Process by placing the jarred preserves into a stockpot of cold water and gradually bringing the water to a low boil; boil for 10 minutes.

Remove the pot from the stove and allow the jars to cool in the processing water.

When they are cooled, remove the jars from the water, wipe dry, and check the lids for a seal after 24 hours. To test, the lid should not flex up and down when the center is pressed.

Store in a cool, dark place for up to 6 months.

Peach Clafoutis & Crème

This baked and fruit-filled custard is light and fluffy. It's traditionally made with cherries, but I like to use whatever fruit is in season, and serve it with a dusting of powdered sugar.

Serves 6

2 tablespoons unsalted butter, room
   temperature
4 large ripe peaches
⅓ cup sugar
½ cup all-purpose flour
⅓ cup sugar
¼ teaspoon salt
4 large eggs, room temperature, beaten
1¼ to 1½ cups buttermilk
1 tablespoon vanilla extract

GARNISH
½ cup heavy cream

Preheat the oven to 350°F.

Butter a large sauté pan and set aside.

Cut the peaches in half and remove the pits. Cut each peach half into 5 or 6 slices and place in a medium bowl, toss with the sugar, and set aside.

In a separate bowl, sift together the flour, sugar, and salt; set aside.

In another bowl, whisk together the eggs, 1¼ cups buttermilk, and the vanilla until light and fluffy. Whisk the flour mixture into the egg mixture until well combined. Whisk in an additional ¼ cup buttermilk if the batter is too thick.

Place the sugared peach slices in the buttered sauté pan about 2 inches apart, and slowly pour the batter around the peaches.

Place in the preheated oven and bake for 45 to 50 minutes, until the clafoutis is fluffy and light golden brown.

Serve Peach Clafoutis in saucers with a drizzle of crème.

BANANA PUDDING

Serves 8

1 cup whole milk
1 cup half-and-half
6 large egg yolks (whites reserved for topping)
1¼ cups sugar, divided
¼ cup all-purpose flour
¼ teaspoon salt
2 teaspoons vanilla extract
1 teaspoon banana extract
50 vanilla wafers
8 bananas, cut into ¼-inch rounds
6 large egg whites

Preheat the oven to 350°F.

In a small stainless steel saucepan over low heat, warm the milk and half-and-half.

While the milk is heating, whisk the egg yolks together with ¾ cup sugar in a large heavy-bottom stainless steel saucepan over low heat for 10 to 12 minutes, until well combined and a light yellow in color.

Stir in the flour and salt and beat until smooth. The egg mixture will be very thick.

Whisk ¼ cup hot milk into the egg mixture to temper the eggs and prevent the yolks from scrambling; slowly whisk in the remaining milk. Whisk for 3 to 5 minutes, until well blended and smooth, then turn the heat to low.

Cook the pastry cream for 5 to 10 minutes, whisking constantly, until it comes to a low boil and is thick and smooth. Add the vanilla and banana extracts and whisk to combine. Strain the pastry cream through a fine sieve into a large bowl and set aside.

Use ⅓ of the the vanilla wafers to cover the bottom of a 9x13-inch baking dish. Spread ⅓ the reserved pastry cream on top of the wafers. Place half of the sliced bananas evenly over the pastry cream and top with a second layer of wafers. Spoon another ⅓ of the pastry cream over the wafers. Top with the remaining wafers, sliced bananas and the pastry cream; set aside.

To make the meringue: Place the egg whites in a large mixing bowl; using an electric mixer fitted with beaters or a whisk attachment, beat the egg whites on high speed until soft peaks form.

Gradually add the remaining ½ cup sugar, 1 tablespoon at a time, beating for 10 to 12 minutes, until stiff peaks form.

Spoon the meringue over the pastry cream and spread evenly with a rubber spatula to cover the entire surface of the banana pudding. Use the spatula to make peaks and swirls in the meringue.

Bake in the preheated oven for 15 to 20 minutes until lightly browned. Remove to a rack to cool slightly.

This Banana Pudding is delicious warm, cold, or at room temperature. It will keep in the refrigerator for 1 week.

How To Make Bananas Foster

1. Melt the butter in a hot pan.

2. Add the sugar and spiices.

3. Add the bananas to the hot sugar.

4. Pour in the rum.

5. Bring the pan to a simmer.

6. Flambé!

Bananas Foster

FLAMBÉ

Serves 8

¼ cup salted butter
1 cup firmly packed brown sugar
½ teaspoon cinnamon
¼ cup banana liqueur
4 bananas, cut in half lengthwise, then
   halved
¼ cup dark rum
8 scoops vanilla ice cream, in individual bowls

Melt the butter in a shallow sauté pan over low heat. Add the sugar and cinnamon and stir until the sugar dissolves.

Stir the banana liqueur into the pan and add the bananas. Cook for 5 minutes, until the bananas soften and begin to brown slightly, then carefully add the rum.

Cook for 2 minutes, until the the rum is hot, then tip the pan slightly to ignite the rum with the stove top flame. If using an electric stove, light a wooden skewer and touch the skewer to the rum sauce.

When the flambé subsides, spoon the bananas over each scoop of ice cream.

Divide the rum sauce between the bowls of bananas and ice cream, and serve immediately.

One of my fondest culinary school memories was being taught how to flambé—making the flaming desserts that were so popular in fancy restaurants. This only happened in the last class of the curriculum, called Restaurant & Buffet. Watching our Chefs show us how to light those classic flaming desserts—Cherries Jubilee, Baked Alaska, and Bananas Foster—appealed to our inner pyromaniacs. If you think about it, these desserts are nothing special; just butter, sugar, and fruit (or ice cream in the case of Baked Alaska)... until you light them on fire and then you have the WOW factor. Imagine it: the smell of browning butter and sugar, a splash of brandy, the tip of the pan and—Whoosh!— flames shooting up and out of the pan, lighting up the dining room and grabbing the attention of every guest there.

This is what every culinary student wanted to do—make their desserts flambé. I remember classmates losing eyebrows and bangs because they added grain alcohol to the brandy in their recipes, all in the quest to get the biggest brightest flames!

DEEP DISH BOURBON PECAN PIE

Serves 8

¾ cup sugar
2 cups dark Karo corn syrup
½ teaspoon salt
1½ teaspoon all-purpose flour
3 large eggs, room temperature
1½ teaspoons vanilla extract
2 tablespoons Bourbon
2 tablespoons unsalted butter, melted
2 cups large pecan halves

PIE CRUST
Yields 1 (9 ½-inch) pie crust

5 tablespoons unsalted butter, cubed
5 tablespoons lard, or substitute shortening
¾ cup cake flour
¾ cup all-purpose flour
1 teaspoon sugar
½ teaspoon salt
⅛ teaspoon baking powder
1 egg yolk
2 teaspoons distilled white vinegar

To make the pie crust: Put the cubes of butter and lard into the freezer for 20 minutes.

In a large bowl, sift together the cake flour, all-purpose flour, sugar, salt, and baking powder. Use a pastry cutter or 2 stainless steel forks to cut the cold butter and lard into the flour mixture, until the mixture resembles peas. Note: Do not over-mix, or your butter and lard will become too warm and your dough too soft.

In a small bowl, mix the egg yolk and vinegar together with 5 tablespoons cold water.

Sprinkle this egg mixture, 1 tablespoon at a time into the dough, adding a total of no more than 4 to 5 tablespoons.

Mix gently with a fork until the dough comes together into a ball. You do not want a wet or over-mixed dough.

Shape the pie dough into a round, thick disk, wrap with plastic wrap, and refrigerate for at least 30 minutes.

Remove the dough from the refrigerator and roll out, on a lightly floured surface, to a 9½-inch circle.

Gently press the circle of dough into a deep 9½-inch pie pan, crimp the edges, and set aside to make your pie filling.

To make the pie filling: Preheat the oven to 350°F.

Using an electric mixer with a paddle or beater attachment, mix the sugar, Karo syrup, salt, flour, and eggs until well combined.

Stir in the vanilla, Bourbon, and melted butter, and pour into the unbaked pie shell.

Cover the mixture with the pecan halves.

Place in the preheated oven and bake for 75 minutes, until a toothpick inserted in the center comes out clean. If the pie crust browns too quickly, cover the edges with aluminum foil.

Transfer the pie to a cooling rack, and let stand at least 3 hours before serving.

Pecan Bread Pudding with *Crème Anglaise*

Serves 8

1 loaf stale French bread, cut into ½-inch
    cubes (about 3 cups)
2 cups sugar
5 large eggs, beaten
1 cup milk
1 cup half-and-half
2 teaspoons vanilla extract
½ cup firmly packed dark brown sugar
¼ cup unsalted cold butter + 2 tablespoons
    butter, softened
1 cup coarsely chopped pecans

CRÈME ANGLAISE
2 cups milk
4 large egg yolks
2 tablespoons cornstarch
6 tablespoons sugar
2 teaspoons vanilla extract
¼ cup Bourbon

Preheat the oven to 350°F.

Butter a 1 (3x9x2-inch) baking dish with 2 tablespoons butter.

Place the cubed bread into the buttered baking dish and set aside.

In a large bowl, mix together the sugar, eggs, milk, and half-and-half. Stir in the vanilla. Pour over the cubed bread and let sit for 10 minutes.

In a separate bowl, mix together the brown sugar, cold butter, and pecans.

Sprinkle the brown sugar pecan mixture on top of the cubed bread and bake for 35 to 45 minutes, until the pudding is golden brown on top and soft in the center.

Set aside to cool while you make the Crème Anglaise.

To make the Crème Anglaise: Pour the milk into a small heavy bottom stainless steel sauce pan on low heat, and cook until hot, but not boiling. Set aside.

In a medium heavy-bottom stainless steel saucepan whisk together the egg yolks, cornstarch, sugar, and vanilla over medium heat.

Whisk in ¼ cup hot milk to temper the egg mixture and keep the egg yolks from scrambling. Slowly pour in the remaining milk, whisking constantly, and cook for 5 to 6 minutes, until the mixture thickens.

Strain through a fine sieve into a medium bowl, and stir in the Bourbon.

Serve warm over the hot Pecan Bread Pudding.

See **Stocking the Perfect Bar**, page 160

★★★
COCKTAILS

Libations

⚜⚜⚜

COCKTAILS
Stocking The Perfect Bar

LIBATIONS

Vodka

Vodka is the workhorse of most bars and is used in basic drinks such as vodka tonics, screwdrivers, and the vodka martini. Like tequila, it is excellent liquor for doing shots, or for mixing into popular cocktails. Vodka doesn't have a strong color, taste, or aroma, so it makes for a perfect liquor for mixers. The differences between vodka brands comes down to what they're distilled from (potatoes, grains, or sugarcane) and the texture of each in the mouth. Some (like Absolut) have an oily, silky texture while others (like Stolichnaya) have a watery, medicinal finish.

Gin

Gin is the perfect clear spirit, and is flavored with juniper berries. It is relatively dry compared with other spirits, and is often mixed with sweeter ingredients, such as tonic water or vermouth, which helps to balance the dryness. The traditional martini is made with gin. It's one of the base spirits for many popular cocktails, so it's good to have plenty on hand. Gin comes in four varieties: London Dry, Plymouth, Old Tom, and Genever. Infused gins are becoming very popular and easier to find, so you may want to stock a cucumber or basil-infused gin along with the traditional brand.

Bourbon whiskey

Bourbon is basically the American version of whiskey, but the big difference is that it is made with at least 51 percent corn, which gives it a distinctive flavor. Great for sipping, and making classic cocktails like the Old Fashioned.

Scotch whiskey

I suggest having a blended and single malt Scotch in your home bar. If you really enjoy Scotch or Irish whiskey, then invest in a good single malt like Glenlivet. Single malt scotch is reserved for those who truly enjoy sipping their drink. For those who consider single malt Scotch too harsh, blended Scotches like J&B and Johnnie Walker Green may go down a bit smoother.

Tequila

Tequila is a must-have liquor for your bar. It's a spirit made from the blue agave plant, a succulent similar to the aloe plant. What type of tequila you stock depends on what you plan on using it for. Gold tequila is usually the less expensive type of tequila, and is perfect for mixed drinks. If you'd like your tequila straight up, you'll want to go with this agave-based drink in its purest form—silver tequila. Tequila has grown exceedingly popular so be sure to have both gold and silver on hand. Like infused gins, infused tequilas are very popular. Try a jalapeño-infused tequila for a spicy shot.

Rum

This tasty liquor from the Caribbean is made from distilled sugarcane, and is perfect for summer cocktails such as daiquiris and mojitos. It can also be served straight or on the rocks. Dark rums are best for punches; light rums are best for mixing cocktails, and served hot in spiced cider. I suggest starting off with both a good quality light and dark rum. What part of the Caribbean your rum is from really depends on how sweet you like it. Mount Gay and Barbancourt have distinctly different tastes, but both are great for sipping and mixing into cocktails.

SPECIALTY LIQUORS

Once your bar is stocked with those essentials, add these specialty liquors:

Vermouth

~A drop of white vermouth, along with gin or vodka, is what makes the martini. To make a Manhattan, add red vermouth.

Orange Liqueurs

~Cointreau and Triple Sec are a distinctive orange-flavored liquors used in margaritas and Cosmopolitans.

Bitters

~Angostura bitters are concentrated bitters that help blend the flavors of many cocktails, including the Old Fashioned and the Manhattan.

GARNISHES

Garnishes add the finishing touch to your drink. The type of garnish you add depends on the drink. Tequila-based cocktails often use citrus garnishes such as a lime or a lemon. Gin-based tonics use olives and onions. Never add garnishes to a Scotch.

Cocktail olives
Cocktail onions
Cornichons
Horseradish
Limes
Lemons
Oranges
Mint leaves
Tabasco sauce
Salt
Pepper
Rimming sugars

GLASSWARE & BAR EQUIPMENT

Martini glasses
Rocks glasses
Highball glasses or tall glasses
Red and white wine glasses
Beer mugs and pint glasses
Martini shaker and strainer
Muddler
Cocktail Spoon
Ice bucket with scoop
Paring knife and cutting board
Wine Key
Beer Key
Toothpicks for the olives and onions
Cocktail napkins

BRANDY CRUSTA

Makes 1 cocktail

2 ounces Cognac
1 teaspoon orange liqueur
1 teaspoon Simple Syrup (recipe, page 178)
2 dashes bitters

GARNISH
1 teaspoon fresh lemon juice
1 tablespoon superfine sugar
1 (3-inch) strip lemon peel

Place the lemon juice in a rimmed saucer.

Prepare a cordial glass by moistening the rim with lemon juice, then dipping it in a saucer of the superfine sugar.

Carefully tuck the lemon peel inside the rim of the glass, curling it as you go.

Combine the Cognac, orange liqueur, simple syrup, and bitters in a shaker with ice and shake vigorously for 10 seconds.

Strain into the garnished glass and add 1 small cube of ice.

The Sidecar

Makes 1 cocktail

¾ ounce orange liqueur
¾ ounce lemon juice
1½ ounces Cognac

GARNISH (optional)
1 tablespoon fresh lemon juice
1 tablespoon superfine sugar
1 (2-inch) strip orange peel

Pour the orange liqueur, lemon juice, and Cognac into a shaker and fill with crushed ice.

Shake for 10 seconds, and strain into a chilled martini glass.

Garnish with the orange peel.

Optionally, you may choose to coat the rim of a chilled martini glass with lemon juice and dip in sugar. If you do so, add the cocktail to the glass after the rim is coated.

BOURBON BLACKBERRY BRAMBLE

Blackberries are a summer staple here in the South. Generally eaten in cobblers and jams, or right off the bush, these berries add a rich sweet-tart taste to cocktails that's hard to resist.

Makes 1 cocktail

½ ounce freshly squeezed lime juice
6 large blackberries
½ ounce Crème de Cassis (blackcurrant liqueur)
½ ounce Simple Syrup (recipe, page 178)
2 ounces quality Bourbon
Club soda

GARNISH
5 Blackberries

Combine the lime juice and blackberries in a rocks glass and muddle until the berries are crushed. Fill the glass with crushed ice.

Combine the Crème de Cassis, simple syrup and Bourbon in a cocktail shaker and shake to combine.

Pour over the muddled berries and crushed ice. Top with club soda.

Stir twice and garnish with the additional blackberries.

The Black Rose

Makes 1 cocktail

2 ounces quality Bourbon
2 dashes bitters
1 teaspoon Blackberry Simple Syrup (recipe, page 179)

GARNISH
1 (2-inch) strip lemon peel
3 blackberries

Fill a cocktail shaker with crushed ice.

Add the Bourbon, bitters, and simple syrup. Shake for 10 seconds.

Pour into a chilled Martini glass and garnish with the lemon peel and blackberries.

KIR COCKTAIL

Kir is a popular French cocktail made with a measure of berry liqueur such as Crème de Cassis (blackcurrant), Crème de Mûres (blackberry), or Crème de Framboise (raspberry); and topped with white wine. These liqueurs are deeply colored, extremely thick and sweet. They are made by macerating the crushed berries in a clear brandy. In France, Kir is usually enjoyed as an apéritif before a meal or snack. Kir Royale is made by replacing the white wine with Champagne, making it more expensive to serve, and is usually reserved for celebrations and special occasions.

Makes 1 cocktail

1 ounce Crème de Framboise
4 ounces dry white wine, such as Chablis, chilled

Pour the Crème de Framboise directly into the bottom of a chilled white wine glass.

Slowly pour in the white wine. The Kir should be a pale pink color—too much Crème de Framboise makes the cocktail too sweet, instead of refreshing.

Kir Royale

Makes 1 cocktail

1 ounce Crème de Framboise
4 ounces brut Champagne, chilled

GARNISH
3 fresh raspberries

Pour the Crème de Framboise directly into the bottom of a chilled Champagne flute.

Slowly pour in the Champagne. The bubbles will help mix the Crème de Framboise and Champagne together.

Garnish with the fresh berries.

OLD FASHIONED

The French may be famous for their cocktails, but the South is infamous for their Bourbon.

Makes 1 cocktail

1 sugar cube
3 dashes Angostura bitters
1 ounce club soda
2 ounces rye whiskey

GARNISH
1 orange slice

Place the sugar cube in an Old-Fashioned glass. Add the Angostura bitters and club soda.

Crush the sugar cube with a wooden muddler and rotate the glass so that the sugar mixture coats the inside of the glass.

Add a large ice cube.

Pour the rye whiskey over the ice cube and garnish with the orange slice.

Sazerac

Makes 1 cocktail

1 teaspoon absinthe
1 sugar cube
2 dashes Peychaud's bitters
1 dash Angostura bitters
2½ ounces rye whiskey

GARNISH
1-inch strip lemon peel

Rinse a chilled old-fashioned glass with the absinthe, add crushed ice and set aside.

In a second old-fashioned glass, add the sugar, both bitters, and 1 teaspoon water.

Crush the sugar cube with a wooden muddler.

Add several small ice cubes and the rye whiskey to the sugar mixture and stir well.

Strain into the chilled old-fashioned glass.

Garnish with a twist of lemon peel.

FRENCH 75

Makes 1 cocktail

1½ ounces gin
¾ ounce fresh lemon juice
1 tablespoon Simple Syrup (recipe, page 178)
1 cup crushed ice
2 ounces dry sparkling wine, well chilled

GARNISH
1 lemon, thinly sliced

Using a zester or paring knife, slice the peel from the lemon in a thin 6-inch long spiral. Curl the lemon peel around your finger to help create the spiral shape; set aside.

Juice the lemon for the cocktail and set aside.

In a cocktail shaker, combine the gin, lemon juice, and simple syrup. Add 1 cup crushed ice and shake vigorously for 20 seconds.

Strain into a chilled Champagne flute and top with sparkling wine.

Garnish with a lemon slice.

White Wine Spritzer

Makes 1 cocktail

2 dashes of lemon bitters
3 ounces white wine, such as Sauvignon Blanc
   or Chardonnay, chilled
1 ounce club soda

GARNISH
1 lemon twist

Pour the bitters into a chilled white wine glass. Add the wine and top with club soda.

Garnish with a lemon twist.

CHAMPAGNE COCKTAIL

Makes 1 cocktail

1 sugar cube
2 dashes Angostura bitters
Champagne, chilled

GARNISH
1 (2-inch) strip orange peel

Place the sugar cube in a chilled Champagne flute and add the bitters.

Top with your favorite Champagne.

Garnish with a twist of orange peel.

Mimosa

Makes 1 cocktail

⅔ cup fresh squeezed orange juice
⅓ cup Champagne, chilled

Pour orange juice into a chilled champagne flute.

Top with your favorite Champagne.

Champagne

Champagne is a region of France, and the only region whose wine can legally be called Champagne. Any other bubbly white wines can only be named "sparkling wines."

SOUTHERN COMFORT COFFEE

Makes 1 cocktail

5 ounces hot black brewed coffee
1 ounce orange liqueur
1 ounce rye whiskey

GARNISH
1 tablespoon whipped cream, recipe follows
1 pinch freshly grated nutmeg

Pour the coffee, orange liqueur and rye whiskey into a warmed coffee mug.
Garnish with the whipped cream and freshly grated nutmeg.

WHIPPED CREAM
Yields about 2 cups

1 cup heavy whipping cream
3 tablespoons powdered sugar
½ teaspoon vanilla extract

In a small chilled copper or glass bowl, beat the cream until it begins to thicken.

Add the powdered sugar and vanilla extract and beat for 10 minutes, until soft peaks form.

Coffee à la Française

Makes 1 cocktail

5 ounces hot black brewed coffee
1 ounce orange liqueur
½ ounce coffee liqueur

GARNISH
1 tablespoon Whipped Cream (see recipe, opposite)
1 teaspoon sugar
1 teaspoon orange liqueur

In a warmed glass coffee cup, pour in the coffee, and the orange and coffee liqueurs.

Garnish by gently floating the whipped cream in the coffee. Sprinkle with sugar and drizzle the teaspoon of orange liqueur on top. Serve immediately.

SWEET TEA COCKTAIL

I came up with this recipe when I needed a Southern inspired cocktail for an event. I used what bits and pieces I had in the liquor cabinet, some leftover orange sugar from a cupcake recipe, brewed some strong tea, and added fresh mint from the garden. Result? A cocktail that is both sweet and refreshing-but beware; it will sneak up on you!

Makes 1 cocktail

2 ounces quality Bourbon
1 ounce Canadian whiskey
1 ounce orange liqueur
1 teaspoon Orange Sugar, recipe follows
4 ounces strong brewed tea
Fresh sprigs mint, for garnish

Combine the Bourbon, whiskey, orange liqueur and Orange Sugar in a highball glass, and stir until the sugar dissolves. Add some crushed ice, top with the brewed tea and garnish with sprigs of fresh mint.

ORANGE SUGAR
2 oranges, zested
1 cup superfine sugar

Place the sugar and orange zest in the bowl of a mini food processor fitted with the blade attachment.

Pulse for 30 seconds, then pour the orange sugar onto a plate. Allow the sugar to dry out for at least 1 hour, then store in a tightly sealed glass jar. Use for cookies and cocktails.

Mint Julep

There's an ongoing debate as to whether the mint in a Mint Julep should be tasted or smelled. Not to worry, when sipping this Mint Julep you'll get the best of both worlds.

Makes 1 cocktail

5 fresh mint leaves
1 tablespoon Mint Simple Syrup, (recipe, page 179)
2 ounces quality Bourbon

GARNISH
1 (4-inch) cocktail straw
1 fresh sprig mint

Place the mint leaves and Mint Simple Syrup in a chilled julep cup.

To release their natural oils, gently crush the leaves against the inside of the cup using the back of spoon.

Pack the cup tightly with crushed ice and pour the Bourbon over the ice. Insert the straw and place a mint sprig next to straw.

SIMPLE SYRUP

Simple is versatile, adding sweetness to cocktails, ice tea, and dessert sauces.

Yields 1 cup

1 cup sugar
1 cup water

In a medium heavy-bottom saucepan, combine the sugar and 1 cup water. Bring to a boil, stirring with a rubber spatula, until the sugar has dissolved.

Reduce the heat to low and simmer for 20 minutes, until the liquid is reduced by half.

Remove from the heat and let it cool. The syrup will thicken as it cools.

BLACKBERRY SIMPLE SYRUP

Yields about 1½ cups

4½ cups blackberries (about 1½ pounds), fresh or frozen
1 cup sugar

Combine the berries, sugar, and ½ cup water in a 2-quart heavy-bottom saucepan over medium-high heat, and bring to a boil, stirring with a rubber spatula until the sugar has dissolved.

Reduce the heat to low and simmer for 30 minutes, stirring occasionally, until the fruit softens.

Pour the mixture through a fine sieve into a medium bowl, mashing the blackberries with the spatula to press the juice through the sieve.

Discard the fruit pulp.

Remove from the heat and let it cool. The syrup will thicken as it cools.

MINT SIMPLE SYRUP

Yields about ½ cup

1 cup sugar
1½ cups fresh mint leaves, firmly packed, and chopped

In a heavy-bottom saucepan, bring the sugar, 1 cup water, and the mint to a rolling boil, stirring until sugar is dissolved.

Reduce the heat to low and simmer for 15 minutes, or until the syrup has reduced by half.

Pour the syrup through a fine sieve, pressing hard on the chopped mint to release all its flavor.

Remove from the heat and let it cool at room temperature. The syrup will thicken as it cools.

BOURBON CHERRIES

Yields about 3 pints

6 cups quality Bourbon
1 cup sugar
6 cups fresh sweet cherries, stemmed and pitted

Combine the Bourbon and sugar in a medium saucepan over low heat. Bring to a simmer and cook for 10 minutes, stirring until the sugar dissolves.

Remove from the heat and let it cool at least 15 minutes. The Bourbon syrup will thicken as it cools.

While the syrup is cooling, tightly pack the cherries into 3 sterilized pint jars, being careful not to crush the fruit.

Pour enough cool syrup into each jar to cover the cherries completely, leaving ¼-inch space from the rim of the jar. Use a sterilized butter knife or wood skewer to gently push the cherries under the syrup, removing any air bubbles.

Screw the sterile lids on the jars, fingertip tight. The cherries will keep in the refrigerator for 1 year.

RECIPE BASICS

BASIC VINAIGRETTE

Vinaigrette is all about the 3:1 ratio. A 3:1 ratio of your favorite oil to vinegar (or other acidic liquids like lemon or lime juice) is pretty standard. The best thing about making vinaigrette—besides how easy it is—is that you can change it to suit your taste.

Yields about 1 cup

¾ cup (or 3 parts) of oil (olive, canola, pecan, or hazelnut)
¼ cup (or 1 part) vinegar (balsamic, cider, red or white wine vinegar; or lemon or lime juice)
1 teaspoon Dijon or whole grain mustard
2 to 3 tablespoons local honey
1 clove garlic, crushed or minced
¼ teaspoon fresh thyme leaves
1 teaspoon finely chopped Italian parsley
Sea Salt and freshly ground pepper, to taste

Whisk the oil and vinegar together in a medium bowl. Add the mustard, honey, garlic, thyme, and parsley and whisk until well combined. Season to taste with salt and pepper.

CHAMPAGNE VINAIGRETTE

Yields 1 cup

1 tablespoon grainy Dijon mustard
1 large garlic clove, minced
1 teaspoon honey
Sea salt and freshly ground pepper, to taste
½ cup Champagne Vinegar (recipe, page 21)
¾ cup extra virgin olive oil

Place the mustard, garlic, and honey in a medium stainless steel bowl.

Stir in the vinegar, and add the oil in a steady stream, whisking until well combined.

The vinaigrette will thicken as you whisk in the oil. Season to taste with salt and pepper.

QUICHE CRUST

Yields 1 crust

1½ cups all-purpose flour
½ teaspoon salt
8 tablespoons cold unsalted butter, cut into
　½-inch cubes

Add the flour, salt and cold butter to the bowl of a food processor; pulse for 2 minutes, until the mixture resembles coarse cornmeal.

While the motor is running, slowly add 4 tablespoons cold water. Pulse until the dough for 30 seconds, until it begins to hold together.

Remove the dough, form into a flat disk and wrap in plastic. Refrigerate for at least 30 minutes, or overnight.

Preheat the oven to 400°F.

Between two pieces of parchment paper, roll out the chilled pastry dough into a 10-inch round. Remove the parchment paper, drape the dough over the rolling pin and transfer to a 9-inch fluted tart pan. Press the dough lightly onto the bottom and sides of the pan; trim and discard any extra dough.

Prick the bottom of the dough all over with a fork, and line with parchment paper and pie weights. Place on a baking sheet and blind bake for 10 minutes. This will keep the crust from bubbling.

Remove the pan from the oven, discard the parchment paper and pie weights and bake for an additional 2 minutes. Remove the quiche shell from the oven and set aside to cool for 30 minutes. This crust can be used immediately or wrapped in plastic and refrigerated for up to 3 days.

QUICK & EASY TART SHELL

Yields 1 tart shell

1 sheet good quality puff pastry, thawed in
　the refrigerator
¼ cup all-purpose flour

Put the oven rack in the middle position and preheat the oven to 400°F.

Lightly flour a work surface and roll the puff pastry into a 10 x13-inch rectangle.

With a sharp knife, evenly cut off the outer 1-inch of all four sides of the puff pastry; try to keep each strip in one piece.

Place the puff pastry sheet in the tart pan. Pierce the pastry all over with a fork.

Using a pastry brush dipped in ¼ cup cold water, brush the top edges of the puff pastry and replace the removed strips of pastry along the edges, pressing firmly to ensure that the pastry strips stick to the sheet of puff pastry.

Place in the refrigerator and chill for 30 minutes.

Remove from the the refrigerator, line with a 10 x13-inch sheet of parchment paper and fill with 2 cups dried beans, or a single layer of pie weights.

Bake 12 to 15 minutes, until the pastry is set and pale golden along the rim.

Carefully remove the parchment paper and dried beans and set the tart shell aside to cool.

REMOULADE SAUCE

Yields about 1 cup

¾ cup mayonnaise
2 teaspoons Dijon mustard
1½ teaspoons whole grain mustard
1 teaspoon tarragon vinegar
¼ teaspoon hot sauce
2 teaspoons drained capers, chopped
1 tablespoon fresh Italian parsley, coarsely
  chopped
1 scallion (3 inches of green left on),
  thinly sliced
Sea Salt and freshly ground pepper, to taste

Combine all the ingredients in a medium bowl.
Season to taste with salt and pepper.

Refrigerate in a covered container. The
Remoulade Sauce will keep in the refrigerator
for 1 week.

MAYONNAISE

Yields about 1 cup

1 large egg yolk, at room temperature
  for 30 minutes
½ teaspoon Dijon mustard
¼ teaspoon fine sea salt, plus more to taste
¾ cup olive or vegetable oil (or a
  combination), divided
1 teaspoon white wine vinegar, or cider
  vinegar
1½ teaspoons fresh lemon juice
Freshly ground white pepper, to taste

In a medium glass bowl, whisk together the egg
yolk, mustard, and salt until well combined.

Add ¼ cup oil drop by drop, whisking constantly for 5 minutes, until the mixture begins to
thicken.

Whisk in the vinegar and lemon juice, then
add the remaining ½ cup oil in a very slow, thin
stream, whisking constantly until well blended.
If at any time it appears that the oil is not being
incorporated, stop adding it and whisk the mixture vigorously until smooth, then continue to
add more oil.

Whisk in the salt and white pepper, to taste.

Chill in a covered container until ready to
use. The mayonnaise will keep in the refrigerator
for 1 a week.

BEEF STOCK

Roasting the beef bones in this recipe intensifies the color and flavor of the stock, adding a robust taste to soups and stews.

Yields about 2 quarts

5 pounds veal or beef bones, cut into 3-inch
  pieces
¼ cup vegetable oil
4 peeled carrots, cut into thirds
4 celery stalks, cut in half
2 unpeeled onions, halved
1 head garlic, halved
1 cup tomato paste
½ bunch flatleaf parsley stems (about 15)
4 sprigs thyme
2 bay leaves
¼ teaspoon black peppercorns

Preheat oven to 425°F.

Place the bones in a roasting pan and coat with oil. Roast the bones for 25 to 30 minutes, turning occasionally, until they are browned.

Add the carrots, celery, onion, and garlic and roast an additional 25 to 30 minutes, stirring occasionally, until the vegetables are dark brown.

Stir in the tomato paste and roast a final 15 to 20 minutes.

Transfer the roasted bones and vegetables to a 6-quart stockpot, and add 5 quarts cold water.

Discard any fat left in the roasting pan, add 1 cup water, and stir; scraping up any browned bits. Add this to the stock pot along with the parsley, thyme, bay leaves, and black peppercorns.

Bring to a boil over medium heat, then reduce the heat to low and simmer for 4 hours, occasionally skimming the foam and fat from the surface. Add additional water as needed to keep the bones covered by at least 4 inches.

Strain the stock through a fine-mesh sieve into a large bowl, discarding any solids.

Cool the stock completely, transfer to a container with a tight-fitting lid, and chill. Refrigerated stock may be kept up to 1 week, or frozen for up to 3 months.

CHICKEN STOCK

Yields about 2 quarts

4 pounds chicken wings, backbones, or carcasses
1 medium onion, unpeeled, coarsely chopped
2 large carrots, peeled, coarsely chopped
2 celery stalks, coarsely chopped
6 sprigs flatleaf parsley
1 teaspoon whole black peppercorns

Combine all the ingredients along with 3 quarts cold water in a large stockpot.

Bring to a boil on medium-high heat; reduce to low and simmer 2½ to 3 hours, until the stock has reduced by one-third. Skim the impurities and fat from the surface of the stock occasionally.

Strain the stock through a fine sieve into a large bowl and discard the solids.

Cool the stock completely, transfer to a container with a tight-fitting lid, and chill. Refrigerated stock may be kept up to 1 week, or frozen for up to 3 months.

VEGETABLE STOCK

Onion skins add a nice rich brown color to vegetable stock, so don't peel them. When making dishes when a lighter colored stock is preferred, like cream sauces, peel and discard the onion peels.

Yields about 2 quarts

1 tablespoon olive oil
2 medium onions, unpeeled, coarsely chopped
10 celery stalks, coarsely chopped
2 large carrots, peeled, coarsely chopped
8 ounces white button mushrooms, halved
1 small fennel bulb, without stems, coarsely chopped
1 head garlic, halved crosswise
6 sprigs flatleaf parsley
1 bay leaf
1 teaspoon whole black peppercorns

In a 6-quart stockpot, heat the oil over medium-high heat.

Add all the remaining ingredients to the pot and cook 5 to 7 minutes, stirring occasionally, until the vegetables begin to soften.

Add 4 quarts cold water. Bring to a boil, then reduce the heat to low and simmer 1 to 1½ hours, until the stock has reduced by half.

Strain the stock through a fine sieve into a large bowl and discard the solids.

Cool the stock completely, transfer to a container with a tight-fitting lid, and chill. Refrigerated stock may be kept up to 1 week, or frozen for up to 3 months.

FISH STOCK

This fish stock is quick, easy, inexpensive, and tastier than any packaged stock you'll find in a store. I double this recipe so I always have some in my freezer for soups and sauces.

1. Sweat the vegetables and the fish.

2. Add the herbs and the wine.

3. Make a parchment paper cover.

4. Cover and sweat the mixture.

Yields about 3 quarts

2 small fish heads (cod or haddock), split lengthwise and gills removed
3 pounds fish bones (sole, flounder, bass, and/or halibut), cut into 2-inch pieces
2 tablespoons olive oil
2 medium onions, very thinly sliced (about 2 cups)
4 stalks celery, very thinly sliced (about 1 cup)
2 medium carrots, very thinly sliced (about 1 cup)
2 dried bay leaves
¼ cup fresh flatleaf parsley, leaves and stems, rough chopped
6 sprigs fresh thyme
2 tablespoons black peppercorns
¼ cup dry white wine
Sea salt

SHRIMP STOCK

Rinse the fish heads and bones of any blood, and set aside.

Heat the oil in a heavy 8-quart stockpot over medium-low heat. Add the onions, celery, carrots, bay leaves, parsley, thyme, and peppercorns.

Sweat the vegetables, stirring frequently, for 10 minutes, until the vegetables become soft and translucent. Do not let them to brown.

Place the fish heads on top of the vegetables and stack the fish bones evenly on top of the vegetables and fish heads.

Add the wine, cover the stock with a piece of parchment paper or a tight-fitting lid, and sweat the bones for 10 to 15 minutes, or until they have turned completely white.

Remove the lid and add enough hot water to barely cover the bones, about 2 quarts. Increase the heat to medium, and bring the pot to a simmer, uncovered, for 10 minutes, skimming off any white foam that comes to the surface.

Remove the pot from the stove, stir the stock, cover with the lid, and let the stock steep for 15 to 20 minutes.

Strain through a fine sieve into a large bowl and season lightly with salt.

As quickly as possible, chill any unused fish stock and transfer it to a container with a tight-fitting lid.

Refrigerated stock will keep for up to 3 days, or frozen for up to 2 months.

Yields about 2½ quarts

2½ pounds shrimp shells, rinsed
1 large onion, peeled and coarsely chopped (about 1 cup)
2 carrots, rough chopped, about 1 cup
2 celery stalks, coarsely chopped (about ½ cup)
2 large cloves garlic, peeled and smashed
1 bay leaf
¼ teaspoon dried thyme
¼ teaspoon black peppercorns
4 stems parsley

Put the shrimp shells in a large 1-gallon stockpot along with 2½ quarts plus 1 cup cold water.

Add the remaining ingredients and bring to a boil over medium-high heat. Reduce the heat to low and simmer for 45 minutes; skimming off any impurities, when necessary.

Remove from the heat and strain the shrimp stock through a fine seive into another large stockpot. Chill the stock immediately by placing the stockpot into an cold bath of water and ice.

Refrigerated stock will keep for up to 1 week, or frozen for up to 3 months.

SOUTHERN SEASONING SALT

Yields about 1 cup

⅓ cup paprika
3 tablespoons dried oregano
3 tablespoons freshly ground pepper
2 tablespoons dried basil
2 tablespoons kosher salt
1 tablespoon cayenne pepper
1 tablespoon granulated onion
4 teaspoons dried thyme
4 teaspoons granulated garlic
1 tablespoon cayenne

Combine all the ingredients in a medium bowl, and stir to combine.

Add to a container with a tight-fitting lid, seal tightly, and shake to combine.

This spice mixture will last up to 3 months when stored in a cool, dark place.

SHRIMP & CRAB PICKLING SPICE

Yields about 1 cup

2 tablespoons whole mustard seeds
1 tablespoon whole allspice berries
2 teaspoons whole coriander seeds
2 tablespoons black pepper corns
1 teaspoon dried mace
1 tablespoon cardamom
1 teaspoon red pepper flakes, or more to taste
1 teaspoon dried ginger
2 dried bay leaves, crumbled
2 cinnamon sticks, crushed
6 whole cloves
2 teaspoons smoked paprika
1 tablespoon celery seed

Combine all the ingredients in a large bowl and stir to combine.

Add to a container with a tight-fitting lid, seal tightly, and shake to combine.

This spice mixture will last up to 3 months when stored in a cool, dark place.

PICKLING SPICE

This mix of dried herbs and spices adds depth of flavor to pickles, pickled fruits, and vegetables.

Yields about 1 cup

¼ cup whole mustard seeds
2 tablespoons whole allspice berries
4 teaspoons whole coriander seeds
¼ cup black peppercorns
2 teaspoons dried mace
2 tablespoons cardamom
2 teaspoons red pepper flakes, or more
   to taste
2 teaspoons dried ginger
4 dried bay leaves, crumbled
3 cinnamon sticks, crushed
10 whole cloves

Add all the ingredients to a glass jar with a tight-fitting lid.
   Seal tightly, and shake to combine.
   This spice mixture will last up to 3 months when stored in a cool, dark place.

BLACKENING SPICE

Add a little heat to your next dinner with this versatile spice—ideal for fish, seafood, and even poultry.

Yields about 1 cup

4 tablespoons sea salt
4 tablespoons freshly ground pepper
2 tablespoon paprika
2 tablespoons cayenne pepper
2 tablespoons garlic powder
2 tablespoons onion powder
2 tablespoon dried thyme leaves

Add all the ingredients to a glass jar with a tight-fitting lid.
   Seal tightly, and shake to combine.
   This spice mixture will last up to 3 months when stored in a cool, dark place.

WHOLE GRAIN MUSTARD

Dijon mustard gets its characteristic flavor from white wine that's added to the mustard-seed soaking liquid. This version has a rustic, grainy texture that adds a pleasant spice to your dishes.

Yields 1 cup

½ **cup dry white wine, such as Sauvignon Blanc**
½ **cup white wine vinegar**
¼ **cup brown mustard seeds**
¼ **cup yellow mustard seeds**
½ **teaspoon kosher salt**

Place all the ingredients in a small, nonreactive bowl and stir to combine.

Cover the bowl tightly with plastic wrap and let it sit at room temperature for 2 days.

Remove the plastic wrap and transfer the mustard mixture to a blender. Blend for 30 seconds, to achieve a coarse texture. (Keep in mind that it's not possible for this mustard to reach a completely smooth consistency.) Transfer the mustard to a small, nonreactive container with a tight-fitting lid, cover, and refrigerate for up to 3 months.

Note: Soak the seeds for 2 days before you blend and serve the mustard. Keep in mind that the oil in the mustard seeds gives them their pungency, and any heat will dissipate over time, so the longer the mustard sits in the refrigerator, the less spicy it will become.

TARRAGON VINEGAR

Yields 1 pint

2 cups white wine vinegar
1½ **cup fresh sprigs tarragon, divided**

Pour the white wine vinegar into a small stainless steel saucepan and bring to a boil over medium-high heat.

Remove from the heat and add 1 cup tarragon sprigs, cover with a tight-fitting lid, and set aside at least 3 hours, or overnight, until the vinegar is completely cool.

Place the remaining ½ cup tarragon sprigs into a sterilized pint jar. Strain the cooled vinegar into the jar, cover with a tight-fitting lid, and discard the old tarragon.

The vinegar will keep in a cool, dark place for up to 3 months.

PEPPERED VINEGAR

Yields 1 pint

1 cup cider vinegar
1 cup white vinegar
1 tablespoon sea salt
½ cup red pepper flakes
3 large garlic cloves, minced

Place both vinegars and the sea salt into a medium saucepan and bring to a boil over medium-high heat.

Remove from the heat and add the red pepper flakes and minced garlic.

Cover with a tight-fitting lid and allow to steep for at least 1 hour.

Pour the peppered vinegar into a clean bottle or jar, seal tightly, and store in a cool place for up to 1 year. The longer the vinegar sits, the more pepppery it will taste.

FOR THE PANTRY

Kosher & sea salt
Black peppercorns
Extra virgin olive oil
Pecan oil
Apple cider vinegar
Balsamic vinegar
Bay leaves
Cayenne pepper
Chili powder
Crushed red pepper
Fennel seed
Cinnamon
Allspice
Nutmeg
Ground ginger
Smoked Paprika
Thyme
All-purpose flour
Granulated sugar
Powdered sugar
Dark brown sugar
Molassas
Honey
Baking soda
Baking powder
Cream of tartar
Cocoa powder
Pure vanilla extract
Beans
Rice
Pasta
Breadcrumbs
Dried fruit
Nuts
White and red wine
Chicken broth
Olives

Capers
Cornichons
Whole peeled tomatoes
Roasted red peppers
Anchovy fillets
Mayonnaise
Dijon mustard
Whole grain mustard
Hot sauce
Worcestershire sauce

KITCHEN CONVERSION

DRY VOLUME MEASUREMENTS

MEASUREMENT	EQUIVALENT
$1/16$ teaspoon	dash
$1/8$ teaspoon	a pinch
3 teaspoons	1 tablespoon
$1/8$ cup	2 tablespoons
$1/4$ cup	4 tablespoons
$1/3$ cup	5 tablespoons + 1 teaspoon
$1/2$ cup	8 tablespoons
$3/4$ cup	12 tablespoons
1 cup	16 tablespoons
1 pound	16 ounces

LIQUID VOLUME MEASUREMENTS

8 fluid ounces	1 cup
1 Pint	2 cups / 16 fluid ounces
1 quart	2 pints / 4 cups / 32 fluid ounces
1 gallon	4 quarts / 16 cups / 128 ounces

EQUIPMENT

This list of essential kitchen equipment will make your cooking experience less like work and more like a culinary adventure!

Mixing bowls, stainless steel, and glass or ceramic
Measuring spoons
Liquid and dry measuring cups
Knives, Chef knife, paring knife, serrated knife, and slicer
Honing steel
Knife sharpener
Cutting board
Rubber and flat spatulas
Wooden spoons
Tongs
Vegetable peeler
Citrus juicer
Firm and balloon whisk
Colander
Fine sieve
Kitchen scissors
Portion scoop
Bottle opener
Wine key
Funnel
Probe thermometer
Stockpot
Saucepan
Sauté pan
Cast-iron skillet
Dutch oven
Grill pan
Roasting pan

Baking sheet pans
Casserole dishes, 8x8-inch and 9x13-inch
Platters
Tart pans
Cake pans
Bread pan
Pie pan
Muffin pan
Rolling pin
Silicone scraper
Ladle
Box grater
Potato masher
Zester
Mixer
Blender
Electric tea kettle
Food processor
Meat grinder
Stick or immersion blender
Can opener
Griddle
Pressure cooker
Assorted canning jars with lids
Timer

COMBINED GROCERY LISTS

Vegetables / Légumes

Pimento Cheese Stuffed Potatoes / Macaroni au Gratin

½ pound thick cut hickory-smoked bacon
1½ cup shredded extra-sharp cheddar cheese
½ cup shredded mild cheddar cheese
4 ounces gruyere cheese
4 ounces cream cheese
1½ cups milk
4 tablespoons unsalted butter
2 cups dried elbow macaroni
2 tablespoons all-purpose flour
½ cup fresh bread crumbs
3 pounds Russet potatoes
1 small onion
1 large garlic clove
⅓ cup diced pimento, or 1 roasted red pepper
½ cup mayonnaise
Pinch fresh grated nutmeg
1 teaspoon smoked paprika
¼ teaspoon cayenne pepper
2 tablespoons kosher salt
1 tablespoon freshly ground pepper

Roasted Beets & Orange Supremes / Roasted Beets with Walnuts, Roquefort & Citrus Vinaigrette

2 ounces Roquefort cheese
8 medium red beets
8 medium golden beets
1 teaspoon local honey
½ cup walnuts halves
3 large oranges
1 large shallot
2 tablespoons white wine vinegar
1 cup extra-virgin olive oil
1 tablespoon sea salt
1 tablespoon freshly ground pepper

Buttermilk Whipped Potatoes / Duchess Potatoes

½ pound unsalted butter
½ cup milk
1 cup heavy cream
1 cup buttermilk
10 large eggs
4 pounds Yukon Gold potatoes
5 pounds Russet potatoes
2 tablespoons salt
¼ teaspoon nutmeg
3 tablespoons kosher salt
2 tablespoons freshly ground pepper

Grilled Summer Zucchini, Squash & Onions / Ratatouille with Fresh Cottage Cheese

1 cup fresh cottage cheese
2 tablespoons apple cider vinegar
1 cup tomato paste
4 large zucchini
6 large yellow crook neck squash
1 small eggplant
1 red bell pepper
1 yellow bell pepper
1 small onion, diced
2 large red onions
2 heads fresh garlic
1 large lemon juice
1 bunch fresh thyme
1 cup olive oil
3 tablespoons kosher salt
2 tablespoons freshly ground pepper
2 cups Vegetable Stock

Baked Omelet with Spring Vegetables / Asparagus & Vidalia Onion Quiche

1 cup shredded Gruyere cheese
1 cup shredded Swiss cheese
½ pound tablespoon unsalted butter
2 cups heavy cream
2 dozen large eggs
2 cups all-purpose flour
2 large Vidalia onions
1 large bunch green onions
2 small zucchini
1 pound fresh thin green asparagus
1 pound fresh thin white asparagus
¾ cup fresh or frozen English peas
1 bunch thyme
1 bunch flatleaf parsley
¼ teaspoon red pepper flakes
¼ cup extra-virgin olive oil
2 tablespoons kosher salt
2 tablespoons freshly ground pepper

Vidalia Onion Tart / French Onion Soup

4 slices thick cut hickory-smoked bacon
4 ounces Parmesan cheese
12 ounces Gruyere cheese
½ cup crème fraîche
½ cup heavy cream
4 large eggs
4 tablespoons unsalted butter
1 sheet good quality puff pastry
½ cup all-purpose flour
1 loaf French bread
2 pounds Vidalia onions
10 ounces Vidalia spring onions
2 pounds yellow onions
1 bunch fresh thyme
⅓ cup olive oil
½ teaspoon freshly grated nutmeg
½ teaspoon ground sage
1 bay leaf
3 tablespoons kosher salt
2 tablespoons freshly ground pepper
6 cups Beef Stock
1 cup white wine
3 tablespoons Cognac

Fried Creamed Corn / Fresh Corn Bisque

6 slices thick cut bacon
4 tablespoons unsalted butter
2½ cups heavy cream
4 tablespoons all-purpose flour
12 ears corn
2 large Russet potatoes,
6 scallions
1 bunch fresh thyme
3 tablespoons kosher salt
2 tablespoons freshly ground pepper

Roasted Sweet Potatoes / Sweet Potato Crepes with Brown Sugar Butter

1¼ pound salted butter
2 large eggs
1 to 1½ cups whole milk
1 cup all-purpose flour
5 medium sweet potatoes
½ cup brown sugar
½ teaspoon vanilla extract
½ teaspoon cinnamon
1 tablespoon vegetable oil or lard
1 teaspoon kosher salt

Braised Collard Greens / Collard Greens Salad with Champagne Viniagrette

4 large bunches collard greens
2 smoked ham hocks
4 ounces salt pork
2 tablespoons white sugar
1 tablespoon apple cider vinegar
2 large red bell peppers
2 large onions
4 garlic cloves
1 cup pecan oil
2 bay leaves
2 ¼ teaspoons red pepper flakes
2 tablespoons sea salt
3 tablespoons freshly ground pepper
½ cup Shallot & Black Peppercorn Vinegar
2 quarts Chicken Stock

Hoppin John and Steamed White Rice / Rice Pilaf with Beurre Noisette

¼ pound thick cut bacon
10 tablespoons butter
1 pound black-eyed peas
1 pound string beans
5 scallions
2 large onions
4 celery stalks
1 small green pepper
3 large garlic cloves
1 bunch fresh thyme
2 bay leaves
1 tablespoon olive oil
3 tablespoons salt
2 tablespoons freshly ground pepper
6 cups Chicken or Vegetable Stock
4 cups Chicken Stock
4 cups long grain rice

Soups, Stews / Potages, Ragoûts

Stewed Tomatoes, Corn & Purple Hull Peas and Succotash with Tarragon & Cräme Fraiche

6 strips thick-cut hickory-smoked bacon
1 cup heavy cream
¼ cup crème fraiche
1 tablespoon unsalted butter
1 pound fresh or dried purple hull peas
2 cups fresh or frozen butter beans
1½ pounds tomatoes
5 fresh ears of corn, or 4 cups frozen corn kernels
3 celery ribs
1 medium red bell pepper
1 large onion diced
1 small sweet onion
4 scallions
5 large garlic clove
1 bunch fresh tarragon
2 tablespoons olive oil
2 tablespoons kosher salt

2 tablespoons freshly ground pepper
8 cups Vegetable Stock

Braised Pig Feet with Hot Peppers / Roasted Pig Feet with Whole Grain Mustard

8 large pig feet, quartered
8 large pig feet, split in half
¼ cup brown sugar
1 cup cider vinegar
3 large ripe tomatoes
5 large onions
6 large garlic cloves
1 head of garlic
1 bunch flatleaf parsley
4 bay leaves
9 dried chili peppers, or 1 tablespoon dried red pepper flakes
2 cups white rice
1 tablespoon Pickling Spice

1 tablespoon sea salt
1 teaspoon freshly cracked black pepper
2½ quarts Vegetable Stock

Crab, Shrimp & Oyster Gumbo / Bouillabaisse

1 pound monkfish
1 pound skinless red snapper fillets
1 pound skinless halibut or sea bass fillets
1 pound Gulf shrimp
8 blue claw crabs
2 cups shucked fresh oysters, with their liquid
2 dozen littleneck clams
2 large eggs
1 loaf French bread
½ cup fresh bread crumbs
¼ cup all-purpose flour
1 tablespoon Dijon mustard
1 large onion (continued on page 196)

2 celery stalks
6 green onions
1 green bell pepper
3 large tomatoes
2 leeks
1 fennel bulb
3 Yukon Gold potatoes
12 large garlic cloves
3 tablespoon filé powder
½ teaspoon saffron threads
8 bay leaves
1 teaspoon dried oregano
1 teaspoon dried thyme leaves
1½ teaspoon cayenne pepper
¼ teaspoon paprika
1½ tablespoon olive oil
¼ cup vegetable oil
4 tablespoons sea salt and
4 tablespoons black pepper
2 quart Fish or Shrimp Stock
6 cups Fish Stock
2 cups long-grain white rice
2 tablespoons Pastis or Pernod

**Pinto Beans & Smoked Ham Hocks /
Cassoulet**

1 pound boneless pork shoulder
6 duck confit legs
3 smoked ham hocks
8 ounces salt pork, with skin attached
1 pound smoked Andouille sausage
2 pound dry pinto beans
¼ cup fresh bread crumbs
1 large onion
1 carrot
1 large tomato
1 whole head garlic
2 large cloves garlic
Bouquet garni
1 tablespoon olive oil
6 cloves
1 cayenne pepper
4 tablespoons kosher salt
4 tablespoons freshly ground pepper
2½ quarts Chicken Stock
10 cups Vegetable Stock

**Summer Vegetable Soup / Soupe au
Pistou**

⅔ cup grated Parmesan cheese
1 cup dried kidney beans
1 cup dried cannellini beans
1 cup dried small pasta, such as orzo,
   or elbow
2 large stalks of celery
4 medium carrots
4 medium zucchini
3 medium Yukon Gold potatoes
1½ pound fresh green beans
12 large ripe tomatoes
2 large ears corn
1 leek
4 large onions
1 head garlic
2 cups fresh basil leaves
1 bunch fresh flatleaf parsley
1 bunch fresh thyme
2 bay leaves
1 cup olive oil
3 tablespoons sea salt
2 tablespoons freshly ground pepper
½ cup Tomato Relish
2 quarts Chicken or Vegetable Stock

Fish, Seafood / Poissons, Fruits de Mer

**Blue Crab & Arichoke Dip /
Artichoke Souffle**

1 pound blue crab crabmeat
¾ cup lump crabmeat
2¾ cups artichoke bottoms
8 tablespoons butter
1 pound cream cheese
1 cup sharp shredded cheddar cheese
1 cup grated Parmesan cheese
½ cup sour cream
1¼ cups whole milk
6 large egg yolks
8 large egg whites
1 lemon
1 red bell pepper
1 bunch green onions
3 large cloves garlic
1 large shallot
1 bunch fresh tarragon
¼ cup mayonnaise

1 teaspoon Worcestershire sauce
5 tablespoons all-purpose flour
1 pinch cayenne pepper
2 tablespoons kosher salt
2 tablespoons freshly ground pepper
¼ cup dry white wine

**Pickled Shrimp & Onions /
Shrimp Creole**

4½ pounds large shrimp, peeled and
   deveined
4 ounces butter
2 tablespoons all-purpose flour
1 cup extra-virgin olive oil
⅔ cups apple cider vinegar
3 large yellow onions
7 large garlic cloves
2 pounds tomatoes
1 large green bell pepper

5 celery stalks
1 large lemon
6 scallions
1 bunch flatleaf parsley
6 dried cayenne peppers
12 dried bay leaves
2 tablespoons kosher salt
¼ teaspoon cayenne pepper
2 bay leaves
1 teaspoons red pepper flakes
½ cup Shrimp & Crab Pickling Spice
1 tablespoon Southern Seasoning Salt
1 tablespoon sea salt
1 tablespoon freshly ground pepper
1 teaspoon Worcestershire Sauce
1 teaspoon hot sauce or Red Pepper Sauce
1 cup Shrimp or Fish Stock
2 cups long-grain white rice

Pan Seared Trout / Poisson au Papillote

1 (2-pound) whole fish, such as snapper, catfish, or trout, cleaned and scaled
6 (8-ounce) trout fillets, skin on
¼ cup unsalted butter
6 tablespoons vegetable oil
1½ cups fresh unseasoned breadcrumbs
4 large Roma tomatoes
1 large red bell pepper
4 lemons
6 large cloves garlic
1 bunch fresh flatleaf parsley
8 fresh sprigs thyme
¼ teaspoon red pepper flakes
½ cup Spanish olives with pimentos
1 tablespoon sea salt
1 tablespoon freshly ground pepper
½ cup olive oil
⅓ cup dry white wine

Seared Salmon Fillets with Fresh Herb Sauce / Salmon Croquettes with Remoulade Sauce

2 pounds salmon
6 (6-ounce) salmon fillets
4 large eggs
¼ cup plain Greek yogurt
¼ cup buttermilk
½ cup fresh bread crumbs
½ cup flour
¼ cup yellow cornmeal
1 medium onion
2 garlic cloves
3 scallions
¼ cup fresh basil leaves
1 bunch fresh flatleaf parsley
1 large lemon juice
2 teaspoons Dijon mustard
½ cup good mayonnaise
½ teaspoon paprika
1 tablespoon kosher salt
1 tablespoon freshly ground pepper
Remoulade Sauce
½ cup good olive oil
½ cup vegetable oil for frying

Pecan Crusted Catfish Fillets / Blackened Catfish with Beurre Blanc Sauce

12 (4-ounce) catfish fillets
3 sticks cold unsalted butter
1 cup milk
2 large egg
1 cup cornmeal
⅓ cup flour
¾ cup pecan halves
2 large shallots
1 fresh lemon
¼ cup white wine vinegar
1 tablespoon salt
1 tablespoon freshly ground pepper
1 teaspoon white pepper
⅓ cup Blackening Spice
1 cup vegetable oil
¼ cup dry white wine

Fried Oysters with Red Pepper Sauce / Roasted Oysters in Champagne

1 pint large Southern oysters, shucked and drained, about 30 oysters
24 fresh oysters, in the shell
2½ cups yellow cornmeal
2¾ all-purpose flour
1 tablespoon Southern Seasoning Salt
1 teaspoon kosher salt
Freshly ground pepper
2 cups rock salt
2 cups buttermilk
¼ cup heavy cream
3 tablespoons salted butter
1 bunch fresh flatleaf parsley
1 bunch fresh thyme
1 bunch fresh dill
½ cup Fish Stock
½ cup brut Champagne

Shrimp & Grits with Tomato Okra Gravy / Shrimp Bouchees

2 pounds large wild caught shrimp peeled and deveined
1 pound small shrimp, peeled and deveined
4 slices thick cut bacon
¾ cup sharp cheddar cheese
¼ cup grated Parmesan cheese
4 tablespoons unsalted butter
1 cup heavy cream
1 sheet frozen puff pastry
1 egg
1 cup yellow stone-ground grits
⅓ cup all-purpose flour
1 small onion
1 garlic clove, minced
10 green onions
2 medium tomatoes
½ pound tender young okra
1 fresh lemon
1 teaspoon Worcestershire sauce
1 teaspoon hot sauce or Red Pepper Sauce
½ cup Vegetable Stock
1 tablespoon Southern Seasoning Salt
1/3 cup olive oil
1 pinch cayenne pepper
1 tablespoon salt
1 tablespoon freshly ground pepper
1 cup Shrimp Stock

Meat, Wild Game / Viandes, Jeu Sauvage

Lamb Shanks with Garlic & Butter Beans and Herb & Dijon Crusted Rack of Lamb

8 lamb shanks
2 French-cut racks of lamb trimmed, about 1½-pounds
2 pounds dried butter beans
1 cup Panko-style breadcrumbs
1 cup olive oil
3 large ripe tomatoes
5 large shallots
12 large cloves garlic
2 bay leaves
8 fresh thyme sprigs
1 bunch fresh mint
1 bunch fresh flatleaf parsley
½ cup tomato paste
4 tablespoons Dijon mustard
1 tablespoon kosher salt
1 tablespoon freshly ground pepper
5 cups Vegetable Stock
4 cups white wine
¼ cup brandy

Pork Chops, Apples & Figs / Pork en Croute with Apple Duxelle

1 (3-pound) pork loin
8 (6-ounce) boneless porkloin chops
1 sheet prepared puff pastry
½ pound unsalted butter
1 large egg
¼ cup all-purpose flour
2 tart apples, such as Granny Smith or Fuji
3 pounds assorted apples
1 small onion
8 large shallots
5 large garlic clove
1 cup fresh orange juice
2 tablespoon olive oil
2 tablespoons red wine vinegar
2 tablespoons cider vinegar
½ cup dried figs
1 tablespoon dried thyme
½ teaspoon crushed aniseed
1 teaspoon crushed fennel seeds
⅓ cup Dijon mustard
3 tablespoons Fig Preserves
1 tablespoon flaked sea salt
1 tablespoon kosher salt

1 tablespoon freshly ground pepper
1 tablespoon freshly ground white pepper
1 cup Calvados

Pulled Pork with Peppered Vinegar / Pork Rillettes

6 pound pork butt, or pork shoulder
2 pounds pork belly
1 pound pork fat
4 onions
8 garlic cloves
¼ cup brown sugar
1 tablespoon chili powder
1 tablespoon smoked paprika
2 tablespoons garlic powder
1 teaspoon cayenne pepper
2 tablespoons kosher salt
2 tablespoons freshly ground pepper
1 Bouquet Garni
6 cups Vegetable Stock

Pot Roast with Root Vegetables / Beef in Red Wine Sauce

6 pounds trimmed beef chuck roast
6 ounces thick cut bacon
3 tablespoons unsalted butter
1 tablespoon all-purpose flour
1 teaspoon sugar
1 tablespoon tomato paste
3 medium onions
1 cup pearl onions
5 large garlic cloves
1½ pound carrots
16 baby carrots
1 pound turnips
2 celery stalks
1½ pounds Russet potatoes
2 cups cremini mushrooms
1 bunch flatleaf parsley
3 sprigs fresh thyme
3 bay leaves
1 tablespoon soy sauce
2 tablespoons olive oil
3 tablespoons kosher salt
2 tablespoons freshly ground pepper
1 cup Beef Stock
1 bottle dry red wine

Chargrilled Steaks with Scallion Butter / Seared Ribeyes with Bernaise Sauce

8 (10-ounce) steaks, ribeye, NY strip, or fillet
8 (1-inch thick) rib eye steaks
4 large eggs
1 pound unsalted butter
2 scallions
3 garlic cloves
3 large shallots
1 bunch fresh tarragon
5 springs fresh flatleaf parsley
½ teaspoon Worcestershire sauce
¼ cup white wine vinegar, or Shallot & Black Peppercorn Champagne Vinegar
¼ teaspoon smoked paprika
2 tablespoons olive oil
¼ teaspoon large grain Sea salt
1 tablespoon kosher salt
2 tablespoons freshly ground pepper
¼ cup dry white wine

Rabbit Roulade with Andouille Dressing / Braised Rabbit with Wild Mushrooms

1 whole rabbit,
2 rabbit loins, or rabbit saddles, deboned
8 slices smoked bacon
1 cup andouille sausage
4 ounces unsalted butter
2 cups cornbread, crumbled
¼ cup all-purpose flour
3 medium onions
4 leeks
8 garlic cloves
2 celery stalks
1 small red bell pepper
¼ cup dry porcini mushrooms
8 ounces cremini mushrooms
4 ounces shitake mushrooms
1 large tomatoes
1 bunch fresh thyme leaves
¼ teaspoon red pepper flakes
3 tablespoons kosher salt
2 tablespoons freshly ground pepper
¼ cup olive oil
1 cup Chicken Stock
1 to 1½ cups Vegetable Stock
½ cup dry white wine

Poultry / Volaille

**Stewed Hen & Fall Vegetables /
Coq au Vin**

1 large stewing hen
4 chicken leg quarters
4 ounces thick cut bacon
6 tablespoons unsalted butter
1½ tablespoons all-purpose flour
4 cups assorted mushrooms, such as
    shitake, or morels
2 cups cremini mushrooms
4 large garlic cloves
4 medium parsnips
4 medium turnips
8 medium carrots
3 large celery stalks
1 medium onion
2 cups pearl onions
½ pound small new potatoes
1 bunch fresh thyme
1 fresh rosemary spring
2 bay leaves
7 cup Chicken Stock
¼ cup tomato paste
4 tablespoon olive oil
2 tablespoons salt
2 tablespoons freshly ground pepper
1¼ cup Cognac, or brandy
½ bottle dry red wine, such as Burgundy

Fried Chicken Liver / Liver Pate

3 pound chicken livers
½ pound salted butter
⅓ cup heavy cream
3½ cups buttermilk
3 large eggs
3 cups all-purpose flour
6 slices white bread
2 medium shallots
1 tablespoon fresh thyme leaves
2 teaspoons cayenne pepper
2 teaspoons ground pepper
1½ teaspoons garlic powder
1 teaspoon paprika
1 tablespoon kosher salt
Oil, for frying
1 teaspoon flake sea salt
¼ cup brandy or Cognac

**Sorghum Glazed Quail and Braised
Quail with Wild Mushrooms & Cognac**

10 whole quail, deboned
4 tablespoons butter
2 tablespoons all-purpose flour
1 tablespoon dark brown sugar
¼ cup sorghum
¼ cup cider vinegar
¾ pound assorted wild mushrooms, such
    as chanterelles, morels, and cremini
4 large shallots
2 large garlic cloves
2 fresh thyme sprigs
1 bunch fresh flatleaf parsley
¼ teaspoon red pepper flakes
⅔ cup olive oil
2 tablespoons vegetable oil
2 tablespoons kosher salt
2 tablespoons freshly ground pepper
1 cup Chicken Stock
½ cup Cognac
1 tablespoon Bourbon

**Southern Chicken Pot Pie / Roasted
Rosemary & Lemon Chicken**

1 (8 to 10 pound) roasting chicken
10 tablespoons unsalted butter
½ cup heavy cream
2 tablespoons cornstarch
2 cups fresh English peas
2 large onions
2 large cloves garlic
1 head garlic
3 medium parsnips
7 medium carrots
5 stalks celery
1 fresh lemon
2 bunches fresh flatleaf parsley
10 stems fresh rosemary
1 bunch fresh thyme
5 tablespoons olive oil
3 tablespoons kosher salt
2 tablespoons freshly ground pepper
2 (9-inch) rounds pie dough
1¾ cups Chicken Stock

**Perfect Pan Fried Chicken / Fried Chicken
Salad with Grapes & Toasted Almonds**

8 fried chicken breasts
½ cup all-purpose flour
2 cups red or green seedless grapes
3 stalks celery
¾ cup slivered almonds
1 cup Mayonnaise
4 teaspoons apple cider vinegar
5 teaspoons honey
2 teaspoons poppy seeds
½ cup vegetable oil
2 tablespoons olive oil
1 tablespoon paprika
2 tablespoons kosher salt
1 tablespoon freshly ground pepper

**Pan Seared Duck Breast with Whiskey
Sauce / Duck Confit and Rendered
Duck Fat**

4 boneless duck breast halves, skin on
4 duck leg and thigh quarters
4 cups rendered duck fat
Skin and fat from 1 whole duck
2 tablespoons butter
1 cup fresh squeezed orange juice
1 large orange
2 shallots
1 tablespoon local honey
¼ cup dark brown sugar
1 bunch fresh thyme
8 large garlic cloves
2 dried bay leaves, broken into small
    pieces
2 tablespoons vegetable oil
3 tablespoons sea salt
1 tablespoon freshly ground pepper
¼ cup whiskey

Desserts / Pâtisseries

Cherry Pie with Chantilly Crème /
Profiteroles with Brandied Cherry
Sauce

2¾ pounds whole pitted dark sweet
   cherries
1/3 cup sweetened cherry juice
3 tablespoons fresh lemon juice
3½ cups all-purpose flour
2 cups sugar
1 cup confectioner's sugar
¾ teaspoon salt
3 tablespoons cornstarch
1 tablespoon arrowroot
¼ teaspoon salt
1½ teaspoon vanilla extract
1 teaspoon kosher salt
2 pounds unsalted butter
6 large eggs
3½ cups heavy whipping cream
¾ cup milk
¼ cup brandy

Apple Spice Cake with Cream Cheese
Frosting / Poached Spiced Apples
with Chantilly Crème

2 cups + 1 tablespoon all-purpose flour
1 teaspoon cinnamon
1 teaspoon nutmeg
1 teaspoon ginger
1 teaspoon allspice
1 cinnamon stick
2 whole star anise
½ teaspoon salt
1¾ cup sugar
6 cups powdered sugar
1 cup dark brown sugar, firmly
   packed
1 teaspoon baking soda
4½ teaspoons vanilla extract
1 cup heavy whipping cream
1½ cup unsalted butter
   + 1 tablespoon
8 ounces cream cheese
4 large eggs
3 large Granny Smith apples
4 Pink Lady or Braeburn apples
½ cup fresh orange juice

1 lemon
1 orange
½ cup raisins
½ cup walnuts, halved
1½ cups fruity red wine, such as
   Syrah or Zinfandel

Lemon Meringue Pie / Tarte au Citron

1½ cups freshly squeezed lemon juice
4 large lemons
14 large eggs
1 pound butter
3 cups sugar
2 teaspoons salt
3½ cups all-purpose flour
1/3 cup cornstarch
1/8 teaspoon cream of tartar

Strawberry Lemon Cake / Frozen
Strawberry Souffle

2½ quarts fresh strawberries
5 cups sugar
4 large eggs
3 ¼ cups cake flour
1 tablespoon baking powder
1 teaspoon salt
2 teaspoons vanilla extract
1 tablespoon powdered gelatin
1 cup milk
3½ cups heavy cream
8 ounces cream cheese
2 large lemons
2 cups Strawberry Lavender Preserves

Shortcake with Peach Preserves /
Peach Clafoutis with Creme

4½ cups all-purpose flour
3 cups sugar
2 tablespoons dark brown sugar
1 cup confectioner's sugar
1½ teaspoons salt
1 tablespoon + 2 teaspoons
   baking powder
1 tablespoon vanilla

4 large eggs
1½ buttermilk
½ pound unsalted butter
3¾ cups heavy cream
4 pounds ripe peaches
1 lemon

Old Fashioned Banana Pudding /
Classic Bananas Foster

1 cup whole milk
1 cup half-and-half
6 large eggs
¼ cup salted butter
1 cup sugar
1 cup brown sugar, firmly packed
¼ cup all-purpose flour
¼ teaspoon salt
½ teaspoon cinnamon
1 teaspoon vanilla extract
Vanilla wafers, about 50
12 bananas
¼ cup Banana Liqueur
¼ cup dark rum
8 scoops vanilla ice cream

Deep Dish Pecan Pie / Pecan Bread
Pudding with Creme Anglaise

3 cups sugar
½ cup dark brown sugar
2 cups dark Karo corn syrup
1 teaspoon salt
¾ cup all-purpose flour
¾ cup cake flour
9 large eggs
3½ teaspoon vanilla extract
3 cups large pecan halves
1/8 teaspoon baking powder
2 tablespoons cornstarch
½ pound unsalted butter
3 cups milk
1 cup half-and-half
5 tablespoons lard
2 teaspoons distilled white vinegar
1 loaf French bread
1/3 cup Bourbon

Cocktails / Libations

Brandy Crusta / The Sidecar

3½ ounces Cognac
2 tablespoons orange liqueur
2 lemons
1 orange
1 tablespoon bitters
2 tablespoons superfine sugar
1 cup white sugar

Bourbon Blackberry Bramble / Black Rose

½ ounce crème de cassis
½ cup good Bourbon
1 tablespoon bitters
2 cups club soda
5 pints fresh blackberries
1 lemon
1 lime
2 cups sugar

Kir Cocktail / Kir Royale Cocktail

1 ounce Crème de Framboise
4 ounces dry white wine, such as Chablis
1 ounce Crème de Framboise
4 ounces brut Champagne
¼ cup fresh raspberries

Old Fashioned / Sazerac

5 ounces rye whiskey
1 teaspoon absinthe
2 tablespoons Angostura bitters
1 tablespoon Peychaud's bitters
1 ounce club soda
1 lemon
1 orange
2 sugar cubes

French 75 / White Wine Spritzer

1½ ounces gin
2 ounces dry sparkling wine
3 ounces white wine, such as Sauvignon Blanc or Chardonnay
2 dashes of lemon bitters
1 fresh lemon
1 cup sugar
1 cup club soda

Champagne Cocktail / Mimosa

1 bottle good Champagne
1 tablespoon Angostura bitters
2 oranges
2 sugar cubes

Coffee a la Francaise / Southern Comfort Coffee

3 ounces orange liqueur
½ ounce coffee liqueur
1 ounce rye whiskey
10 ounces hot black brewed coffee
1 cup heavy whipping cream
3 tablespoons powdered sugar
½ teaspoon vanilla extract
1 pinch fresh grated nutmeg

Sweet Tea Cocktail / Mint Julep

4 ounces good Bourbon
1 ounce Canadian whiskey
1 ounce orange liqueur
1 teaspoon Orange Sugar
½ cup strong brewed tea
2 cups fresh mint springs
2 oranges
1 cup superfine sugar
1 cup white sugar

Glossary

Bouillabaisse: a soup or stew, originally from Provence, made of several different kinds of fish and shellfish, usually combined with olive oil, tomatoes, and saffron.

Braising: a cooking technique which browns the main ingredient in hot fat, and then simmers it in liquid, in a pot with a tight fitting lid. *Beurre Noisette: a sauce of butter cooked until golden or 'hazelnut' brown, usually flavored with capers, herbs, or vinegar.*

Cassoulet: a rich, slow-cooked casserole originating in the south of France, typically containing pork sausages, goose, duck, sometimes mutton, pork skin and white beans.

Chiffonade: a French chopping technique in which leafy herbs or vegetables are stacked, rolled tightly, and sliced into long, thin strips resembling confetti.

Confit: usually prepared from the legs of ducks or geese. The meat is salted and seasoned with herbs, and slowly cooked submerged in its own rendered fat; traditionally cooled and then stored in the fat.

Crème Anglaise: a French term used to describe a light custard sauce that is made of egg yolks, sugar, hot milk, and cream; and served on French desserts such as bread pudding.

Deglaze: to delgaze means to add liquid, such as stock or wine, to a hot pan to loosen and dissolve food particles (called fond) that are stuck to the pan. It can then be used to make a sauce.

En Croute: a savory food that has been wrapped in pastry dough, then baked in the oven.

Lardons: generally fatty bacon or pork fat, cut into ¼ x 1½-inch strips and cooked to remove the fat. They are used to add fat or tenderize dishes, and to add flavor and moisture to tough, dry cuts of lean meat as the meat cooks.

Meringue: a whipped topping created with egg whites and sugar, beaten until they are stiff enough to form peaks and baked on pies, puddings, and cookies.

en Papillotes: a French term meaning "in paper" which is used to describe the technique of placing food on parchment paper or aluminum foil, sealing it, and then cooking the contents. This process steams the food inside, resulting in a moist and juicy dish.

Pistou: a Provençal cold sauce made from garlic cloves, fresh basil, and olive oil. It is similar to a pesto, but without the pine nuts.

Rillettes: a pâté made of minced pork or other light meat, highly seasoned; and combined and sealed with fat.

Rouille: a French term meaning "rust" that describes the burnt red colored sauce made from chili peppers, garlic and olive oil. This spicy sauce is served most often with bouillabaisse.

Roux: a thickening agent made from equal weight of fat and flour, cooked together, and used to thicken sauces, gravies, and soups.

Tarte: a French term for an open pastry 'tart' that contains sweet or savory ingredients.

Trussing: to tie meat or poultry with a string in order to make the meat more compact. Typically, the wings and legs of poultry are tied or trussed securely against the body to keep them from opening during cooking and makes for a more even cooking.

INDEX

ACKNOWLEDGMENTS

I have had so much fun writing *Dinner Déjà Vu*! A big hug and kiss to all of you who have helped me along this cookbook journey, through encouraging words, sage advice, moving props, grocery store runs, and washing lots and lots of dishes!

My daughters, Jenelle and Regine, thank you for picking up the slack so that Mommy could write this book. You girls are my daily inspiration and motivation—I love you!

My sisters, Naomi and Erin, who are and have always been my biggest cheerleaders—that means everything to me.

Thank you, Michelle, for all that you do everyday to help me make my dreams come true!

Thanks to Cook's Warehouse for your generosity, encouragement, and support. You Rock!

Many thanks to Hammer Stahl for the use of your beautiful cookware and exquisite knives. They made cooking my dishes a joy.

Many thanks to Clay Oliver of Oliver Farms, and his lovely family, for supplying me with endless bottles of his Pecan Oil. Yours really is the best.

Tamiera McNeil, your help on the set, your keen eye for style and endless ice coffees made my job easier, and I thank you.

My 'Pink Posse' sous-chef, Pier Durst, I appreciate your willingness to pack your knives, apron and pearls and travel the world with me.

Dianna Smith Gehrich, thank you for endless hours talking food, recipe testing, and listening to me laugh and cry (and sometimes yell), over this book.